DiaPhon 2

Diagnostic Phonics/Spelling Support Pack

Diagnostic assessment and worksheets in phonics and spelling

Adrienne Stevens

Hodder & Stoughton
A MEMBER OF THE HODDER HEADLINE GROUP

The author

Adrienne Stevens' experience of special needs teaching spans more than thirty years and includes time spent in multi-racial comprehensive schools in socially deprived areas in the north and south of England, a Community Home School for Senior Girls, a boys' Remand Centre, ESL work, setting up and running a department for children statemented to have a variety of special educational needs within a large comprehensive school, and work within the private sector of education. She holds an RSA Diploma in SpLD and is an active member of the Professional Association of Teachers of Specific Learning Difficulties (PATOSS).

Acknowledgements

DiaPhon was a working document before publication was considered. An Educational Psychologist friend and former colleague, Mike Lake, suggested that the material should be developed to enable it to be used by other teachers.

I would like to acknowledge the inspiration I received from the work of Beve Hornsby, Kathleen Hickey, Violet Brand, Marie Clay and Marilyn Jager Adams. Thanks are also due to the RSA Diploma course tutors whose enthusiasm, knowledge and patience provided me with a new way of looking at special educational needs.

I am grateful for the support of teaching colleagues, learning support assistants, pupils and parents who have taken part in trials of the material which has made the task of developing the document that much easier. Charles Knight from Hodder Headline has been supportive throughout and I would like to thank him for the courtesy, time and patience he has expended on helping me structure the work to make it more accessible for use by others.

I would also like to thank friends and family who have encouraged me throughout the project. Most of all, thanks must go to my husband, who has steadfastly believed in **DiaPhon** and whose support has enabled me to concentrate on finishing it.

Adrienne Stevens

Orders: please contact Bookpoint Ltd, 130 Milton Park, Abingdon, Oxon OX14 4SB. Telephone: (44) 01235 827720, Fax: (44) 01235 400454. Lines are open from 9.00 – 5.00, Monday to Saturday, with a 24 hour message answering service. You can also order through our website: www.hoddereducation.co.uk

A catalogue record for this title is available from The British Library

ISBN-10: 0 340 77146 1
ISBN-13: 978 0 340 77146 4

First published 2000
Impression number   10 9 8 7 6
Year   2008 2007 2006

Designed and typeset by Ian Foulis & Associates, Plymouth, Devon
Printed in Great Britain for Hodder Education, a division of Hodder Headline, 338 Euston Road, London NW1 3BH, by Hobbs the Printers, Totton, Hants.

Introduction

What is DiaPhon?

DiaPhon is an integrated resource of phonics and spelling activities accessed via diagnostic assessment. Work is sharply focused, allowing both pupil time and teacher time to be utilised effectively. Straightforward recording makes for easy manageability and planning.

DiaPhon enables a special needs coordinator or literacy support teacher to establish the point an individual pupil has reached in phonic awareness and spelling, and to identify learning needs. The work is presented in a carefully structured form, with content and vocabulary appropriate to pupils aged 8 to 15.

- **DiaPhon 1** reflects the teaching sequence of the specific phonics and spelling work recommended in the National Literacy Strategy – a sequence which is equally applicable to older pupils.
- **DiaPhon 2** progresses to work on more vowel digraphs, non-phonically regular letter clusters, plurals, suffixes, silent letters, etc. Here, the ordering reflects acknowledged good practice and extensive experience of what works with pupils needing literacy support.

How DiaPhon works

In each Pack, a *Diagnostic Spelling Test* assesses applied knowledge of sound/symbol relationships and patterns of spelling, to identify the sounds, letters and letter strings which the pupil has still to master, and any pattern of difficulties which may point to specific problems. Parallel tests allow pupils to be re-tested at a later date in order to monitor progress.

From the test, a *Spelling Matrix* identifies the most appropriate of 80+ photocopiable worksheets in each Pack, to match teaching material to the individual pupil's immediate learning needs. It is not intended that every pupil should work through every worksheet! Teacher preference for order of working may also be exercised. The matrix serves as an individual pupil record on which to plan and set targets for future learning.

The worksheets provide opportunities for reading, writing, comprehension and language development based on the application of phonics and spelling rules, as well as structured work on the target letter string. Above all, **DiaPhon** leaves the teacher free to teach, because the source material and means of accessing it efficiently are provided.

The sequence, sheet numbers and content of the worksheets can be viewed on the matrix in each pack.

Overview

DiaPhon presents opportunities for developing phonic skills and spelling strategies in a variety of ways, in order to maintain pupil interest and to utilise individual strengths. The work is teacher-led, and it is essential that a small-steps approach is used. It is not intended that pupils should work through the sheets without close supervision. A multi-sensory approach to the tasks is encouraged by the form of instruction given on the worksheets.

The structured approach enables the teacher to set realistic targets for each pupil. The matrices provide an easily-viewed record of the pupil's attainments and future goals, and the small-step formula has a proven record of success in terms of motivating pupils. They can see on the matrices what has been mastered and what remains to be done. The parallel test gives concrete evidence of progress or the need for continued effort.

Photocopiable worksheets with clear instructions make it easy to involve parents in homework tasks. The matrices provide a record of work done, whether it is completed at home or in school, and provide a sound basis for effective parental communication and support.

Using DiaPhon

To assess a pupil successfully, it is necessary to establish a working relationship. It will be useful to spend a few minutes explaining to the pupil why you are going to test/observe their work and how you are going to do it. It is also a good idea to discuss the test procedure and marking system with them: this helps to make the pupil feel more in control and less nervous, particularly if the tester is unfamiliar. Emphasise that the point is to find out what they do know and how they work, so that they can be helped without wasting time on things they can do already. Show them the matrix and explain its purpose.

If a spelling age is available, use **DiaPhon 1** for pupils with a spelling age up to 10 and **DiaPhon 2** for a spelling age of 10+. If chronological age is the only guideline available, teacher judgement based on observed spelling behaviour in the classroom will be required.

The tests may be administered in one session or in stages. The test words are grouped in units of five for ease of administration. On any one occasion, stop testing after the pupil has made five consecutive errors.

Diagnostic Spelling Test A

Provide the pupil with a sheet of A4 lined paper and a pen (a computer may be used if the pupil's handwriting skills are very weak). Tell the pupils you want them to do their very best to spell correctly each of the test words you will read aloud. Read each word aloud twice and put it into a phrase or sentence to facilitate comprehension. This is particularly important in the case of homophones. Read from left to right. The target onsets, rimes and letter strings are shown in bold. For items 1 and 40, the pupil is asked to divide the word into syllables.

Record results on a photocopy of the Test sheet or directly onto the *Spelling Matrix* using a tick for each correct response in the designated box. A gap will indicate an incorrect response and a need for further work on the target letter string: the number below each test item and in the corresponding box in the *Spelling Matrix* refers to the appropriate worksheet for follow-up.

Work on the areas of weakness using the appropriate worksheets; re-test using *Diagnostic Spelling Test B*. Once the pupil has mastered the spelling patterns to the point at which testing was discontinued (i.e. when five consecutive errors had been made), proceed with the next group of words, repeating the previous process until all items on the matrix have been mastered.

Diagnostic Spelling Test B

Explain that the purpose of the second test is to check if the pupil has learnt what they have been taught and to help in setting the next target.

Follow instructions as for *Diagnostic Spelling Test A*, above. If errors are repeated in the second test, further work on the target letter string is desirable: continue with the next stage of *Diagnostic Spelling Test A*.

The Spelling Matrix

When the results of the tests have been plotted on the *Spelling Matrix*, it sometimes becomes obvious that difficulties are confined to a particular pattern of letter strings, for example consonant blends or word endings. This section of work should be taught as a priority and a random spelling test given using words from the worksheets. The pupil can receive a confidence boost if results indicate that a lack of knowledge was caused by circumstances, such as a long illness or a specific difficulty such as a temporary hearing impairment brought about by a severe cold, rather than lack of ability.

Use of the tests and matrices has revealed that the normal picture of the completed matrix shows random gaps followed by a continuous progression of gaps. Work first on the random gaps in knowledge, in order to secure the foundation for future work.

It is useful to have some idea of a pupil's speed of working and rate of progress in order to set realistic goals. One way of tracking this is to use a different coloured pen to mark on the matrix the work completed during, say, each month or term, and to use this to target future progress, taking into account any specific learning difficulty. Relatively non-productive periods are then highlighted and provide a basis for discussion with pupil and parents.

Intervention: using the worksheets

The **DiaPhon** worksheets have been designed to provide opportunities for more than simply practising letter strings. The variety of exercise types on each sheet aids motivation, provides differentiated work, encourages multi-sensory learning and enables diagnostic teaching to take place. The instructions for work vary from exercise to exercise and from one worksheet to another. This is to encourage the pupil to develop good working practices by ensuring that successful outcomes can only be obtained by reading the instructions carefully and interpreting them accurately. If errors in carrying out the instructions are noted, work on comprehension and study skills should be introduced into the pupil's Individual Education Plan (IEP), as targets.

In **DiaPhon 2**, most of the target words are multi-syllabic. Worksheet 1 provides basic work on syllables, and this is expanded upon in Worksheet 40. Clapping out the number of syllables in words throughout **DiaPhon 2** is helpful, especially for pupils with poor auditory skills.

Look, say, cover, write and check is the suggested method for practising specific letter strings. Where space on the worksheet allows, up to three repetitions are envisaged to help develop kinesthetic memory. If visual processing is weak, errors are sometimes made on the second or third repetition. This can be pointed out to the pupil and the need for vigilance in checking stressed. The use of simultaneous oral spelling can be introduced to help overcome the visual weakness, especially if auditory sequential memory is good. The 'boredom' factor has not reared its head in my experience. If it does, the activity can be broken into two or more sessions.

'**Target words**' (shown in boxes on the worksheets) are deliberately not presented in a particular order. The idea is for the pupil to search for them, actively scanning, if not consciously reading each one, as they work through the exercises. Suggestions for extension studies could, however, include asking pupils to order them alphabetically to develop sequencing skills, or order them according to the number of letters to practise visual processing.

Opportunities for **dictionary work** are included. This can be used as an extension activity for the pupil who works quickly, as a vocabulary extending exercise, and a way of checking if the pupil can use a dictionary efficiently. The concept of a root word with different suffixes creating different parts of speech can also be demonstrated as a by-product of the dictionary tasks.

If the task is inappropriate because of the age or ability of the pupil, it can be omitted or the teacher or a fellow pupil can supply the information. If dictionary skills are observed to be weak, remedial activities can be included as targets in the pupil's IEP.

Visual and auditory skills are referred to specifically in some exercises, such as tracking and word searches, and discriminating between the sounds of '*f*' and '*v*' in plural work. Teacher choice can be exercised if such work is deemed unsuitable for a particular pupil because of a specific learning difficulty. In some cases, the practice given can strengthen weak areas of processing.

Cloze passage work is provided to check that pupils understand the meaning of the words they are learning to spell, as well as helping to develop syntactic skills. An extended vocabulary is used, particularly in **DiaPhon 2**, in order to give the pupil experience of as wide a range of words as possible.

The **free-writing** activities provide opportunities for the pupil to demonstrate comprehension, knowledge of sentence structure, punctuation and handwriting skills. The teacher has a current record of the pupil's written communication skills and can use them to monitor progress as well as identify strengths/weaknesses for use in setting IEP targets. Sometimes, it is necessary to work out of order of sequence, to respond to an individual's needs exposed by the free-writing work. The matrix enables this to be recorded for future reference. (A useful alternative way of utilising the free-writing activity space is to ask the pupil to *dictate* their responses to a teacher, parent or learning support assistant: this is particularly useful where speed of written output is slow or handwriting illegible.)

Short **tracking** exercises are included on some worksheets. They can be used as dictation passages if this is a more appropriate activity for the pupil. If these are used for dictation, it is helpful to allow pupils to read the passage first in order to revise non-target words, to provide reading practice and to check that the pupil comprehends the vocabulary.

Computer skills can be encouraged by using word processing for dictation work and free-writing activities. Self-correction can take place whilst proofreading skills are exercised in a realistic situation. Computer-literate pupils may also create additional worksheets of their own by producing crosswords from the lists of target words: several software packages available offer a crossword facility. This type of creative work is useful for the bright pupil with a specific learning difficulty. It gives a boost to self-esteem and adds to resources.

Diagnostic Spelling Test A

Date _____

Name _____

Procedure: Provide the pupil with a sheet of A4 lined paper and a pen. Tell the pupil you want them to do their very best to spell correctly each of the test words you will read aloud. Read each word twice and put it into a phrase or sentence to facilitate comprehension. Read from left to right. The target onsets, rimes and letter strings are in bold. Record results on a photocopy of this sheet or directly onto the **DiaPhon 2** *Spelling Matrix*. The number below each test word identifies the relevant worksheet.

It is *not* necessary to give the whole test on a single occasion: discontinue each testing session after the pupil has made five consecutive errors.

des / troy 1	**strain** 2	**qu**iet 3	**want** 4	**squa**sh 5
swarm 6	**wor**se 7	cha**lk** 8	flask 9	rather 10
do**dge** 11	stre**tch** 12	son 13	glove 14	th**row** 15
gr**ou**p 16	bl**ind** 17	beach 18	ri**ot** 19	trot**ted** 20
liv(**e**)ing 21	hopeful 22	mana**geable** 23	pretti**ly** 24	play**ing** 24
trave**lled** 25	table**s** 26	tax**es** 27	gyps**ies** 28	photo**s** 29
volcano**es** 29	roof**s** 30	lea**ves** 30	women 31	**kilt** 32
stuck 33	jackal 34	suc**cess** 35	**g**inger 36	caravan 37
remem**ber** 38	**haunt** 39	in / div / id / u / al 40	already 41	expe**lled** 42
ac**cu**se 43	usua**lly** 44	ques**tion** 45	correc**tion** 45	gig**gle** 46
terri**ble** 46	fav**our** 47	**ch**aos 48	ma**ch**ine 49	anti**que** 50
autogra**ph** 51	**ph**ysical 51	cou**gh** 52	**centi**pede 53	thief 54
wei**g**ht 55	musi**ci**an 56	occa**sion** 57	discu**ssion** 58	curious 59
immed**i**ate 59	un**sure** 60	arch**ery** 61	allow**ed** 62	**ore** 62
knight 63	plum**ber** 64	answer 65	build 66	**hymn** 67
alth**ough** 68	**cen**tury 69	band**age** 70	**anti**septic 71	gener**ous** 72
par**tial** 73	ignor**ance** 74	complim**ent** 75	merely 76	**yach**t 76

Diagnostic Spelling Test B

Date

Name_____

Procedure: Provide the pupil with a sheet of A4 lined paper and a pen. Tell the pupil you want them to do their very best to spell correctly each of the test words you will read aloud. Read each word twice and put it into a phrase or sentence to facilitate comprehension. Read from left to right. The target onsets, rimes and letter strings are in bold. Record results on a photocopy of this sheet or directly onto the **DiaPhon 2** *Spelling Matrix*. The number below each test word identifies the relevant worksheet.

It is *not* necessary to give the whole test on a single occasion: discontinue each testing session after the pupil has made five consecutive errors.

em / ploy 1	sprain 2	quench 3	wand 4	squat 5
warn 6	worship 7	stalk 8	last 9	father 10
hedge 11	fetch 12	front 13	stove 14	grow 15
mould 16	grind 17	beach 18	violent 19	cleaned 20
sav(e)ing 21	safely 22	peaceable 23	beautiful 24	enjoyed 24
wheeled 25	roses 26	benches 27	monkeys 28	discos 29
potatoes 29	scarfs 30	loaves 30	mice 31	kidnap 32
flock 33	jumper 34	accident 35	garage 36	cardigan 37
shepherd 38	launch 39	in / sti / tu / tion 40	joyful 41	feeling 42
cunning 43	annually 44	section 45	prescription 45	middle 46
possible 46	glamour 47	choir 48	avalanche 49	unique 50
phantom 51	nephew 51	tough 52	microscope 53	relief 54
reign 55	official 56	invasion 57	admission 58	serious 59
brilliant 59	figure 60	primary 61	hoarse 62	oar 62
knuckle 63	crumb 64	folk 65	guessed 66	autumn 67
nought 68	excellent 69	average 70	misbehave 71	precious 72
special 73	extravangant 74	difference 75	weird 76	jewellery 76

Spelling Matrix

DiaPhon 2 Date of birth _____

Name _____

School _____ Class _____

Test: ✔ if correct	✔	Worksheet	Date	Test: ✔ if correct	✔	Worksheet	Date	Test: ✔ if correct	✔	Worksheet	Date
Syllables		1		Plurals 2 -**es**		27		**gh** *saying 'f'*		52	
ain		2		Plurals 3 -**y**		28		Prefixes and suffixes		53	
qu		3		Plurals 4 -**o**		29		**ie** *saying long 'e'*		54	
wa *saying 'wo'*		4		Plurals 5 -**f/-fe**		30a/b		**ei** *saying 'ay'*		55	
qua *saying 'quo'*		5		Plurals 6 - irregular words		31		**ti/ci** *saying 'sh'*		56	
war *saying 'wor'*		6		**k-**		32		-**sion** *saying 'shun'*		57	
wor *saying 'wer'*		7		-**k**		33		-**ssion** *saying 'shun'*		58	
al *saying 'aw'*		8		**j-**		34		Short **i**		59a/b	
a+s *saying 'ar'*		9		Soft **c**		35		**ure** words		60	
a+th *saying 'ar'*		10		Soft **g**		36		-**ery/-ary/-ory**		61	
dge		11		More **ar** words		37		More homophones		62a/b	
tch		12		**er**		38		Silent **k** and **g**		63	
o with short '*u*' sound		13		**au**		39		Silent **b** and **h**		64	
The **v** rule		14		More syllables		40		Silent **w** and **i**		65	
Long '*o*' spelt **ow**		15		**ll** in compound words		41		Silent **u** and **t**		66	
'*ou*' sounds		16		**ll** + **ing** and **ed**		42		More silent letters		67	
Long vowel – no magic **e**		17		Double letters-2/3 syllable words		43		**ough**		68	-
ee & **ea** homophones		18		Double letters 2 -**lly**		44		More soft **c**		69	
ia, ie, io		19		-**tion** *saying 'shun'*		45a/b		More soft **g**		70	
Suffixing 1 '123 rule'		20		-**le**		46a/b		More prefixes and suffixes		71	
Suffixing 2 (magic **e**)		21		**our** *saying 'er'*		47		-**ous/-ious**		72	
Suffixing 3 (+ consonant)		22		**ch** *saying 'k'*		48		-**tial/-cial**		73	
Suffixing 4 (-**able**)		23		**ch** *saying 'sh'*		49		-**ance/-ant**		74	
Suffixing 5 (-**y**)		24a/b		**que** *saying 'k'*		50		-**ent/-ence**		75	
Suffixing 6 (-**l**)		25		**ph** *saying 'f'*		51a/b		Tricky words		76	
Plurals 1 -**s**		26									

DiaPhon 2 published by Hodder & Stoughton Educational.
The publishers grant permission for photocopies of this sheet to be made for use solely in the purchasing institution.

Syllables

Things you need to know when talking about syllables:

1. All words or syllables within words contain at least one vowel (or 'y').

2. An OPEN syllable ends in a vowel which has a long sound – e.g. *de / light.*

3. A CLOSED syllable ends in a consonant and also has a short vowel sound – e.g. *cap / tain.*

4. You need to be able to talk about syllables because as you read and spell longer words, you will find it easier if you can break them into syllables. You will find that many words which look difficult are easy when you divide them into syllables.

Open **syllables end in a vowel – the vowel has a long sound.**

For example: acorn   a / corn   humid   hu / mid

Divide these words into syllables as shown in the examples.

label _____   even _____

crocus _____   Roman _____

pupil _____   stupid _____

robot _____   private _____

• •

Closed **syllables have short vowels.**

For example: dentist   den / tist   magnet   mag / net

Divide these words into syllables as shown in the examples.

intend _____   pistol _____

flannel _____   splendid _____

velvet _____   disgust _____

window _____   infant _____

perhaps _____   kidnap _____

It is much easier to spell and read long words if you break them into syllables.

DiaPhon 2 published by Hodder & Stoughton Educational.
The publishers grant permission for photocopies of this sheet to be made for use solely in the purchasing institution.

Words containing 'ain'

A number of words contain the letter string 'ain'.
If you add a prefix to this letter string, you can form many words.

For example: 'g' + 'ain' = _gain_

Add these prefixes to 'ain'. Read aloud the words you have made.

'gr' 'r' 'str' 'p' 'br' 'dr' 'tr' 'spr' 'cont' 'expl' 'rem' 'obt'

_____ _____ _____

_____ _____ _____

_____ _____ _____

_____ _____ _____

Use some of the words you have made to complete these sentences.

1. I went to the bank to _____ a cheque book.

2. If you lift a heavy weight you may _____ your back.

3. I had a _____ in my side from laughing too much.

4. The road flooded because the _____ was blocked.

5. I will always _____ your friend.

6. I asked the teacher to _____ the method again.

Make word families from the root word.

For example: rain rained raining

contain _____ _____ _____

strain _____ _____ _____

train _____ _____ _____

drain _____ _____ _____

chain _____ _____ _____

obtain _____ _____ _____

remain _____ _____ _____

'qu' words

Say the 'qu' as *kw* in these words. Read the sentences aloud, then look, say, cover, write and check the words shown below.

Ducks can quack quite quickly.   The patchwork quilt was quite beautiful.
Quench your thirst with Quentin's squash.   A quick quiz is over quickly.

quiet _____   quick _____   quilt _____

queen _____   quack _____   quench _____

qualify _____   quality _____   quantity _____

quarrel _____   equal _____   quarter _____

quite _____   questions _____   qualification _____

In this group of words, the 'qu' sounds like 'k'.
Read the words aloud and listen to the sound.

| cheque | antique | technique | queue | conquer | mosquito |

Look, say, cover, write and check the *kw* sound in these words with middle 'qu'.

equality _____   inquire _____

aquarium _____   equator _____

earthquake _____   require _____

inquisitive _____   request _____

equipment _____   liquid _____

enquiries _____   equals _____

Use the correct word from the words above to complete the sentences. You may need to ask for help.

1. The police are making _____ into the burglary.

2. One and one _____ two.

3. A mouse is an _____ animal.

4. The _____ destroyed many buildings.

5. Water is a very important _____.

6. Have you collected all the _____ for the experiment?

7. I made a _____ for a record to be played on the radio.

8. You need to keep tropical fish in an _____.

DiaPhon 2 published by Hodder & Stoughton Educational.
The publishers grant permission for photocopies of this sheet to be made for use solely in the purchasing instituion.

3

'wa' saying '*wo*' with a short sound

Read these List 1 words aloud.

List 1	was	want	what	wash	was	wand	whatever

Fill in the words *want* or *what* in the correct spaces in these sentences.

1. _____ I would like for Christmas is a secret.

2. _____ do you _____ that for?

3. _____ did you say?

4. I don't _____ any of that, thank you.

5. _____ is the good of working so hard?

6. _____ a lovely day out we had!

· ·

Read the List 2 words aloud. Find out the meanings of any you don't know. Use the words from lists 1 and 2 to make sentences.

List 2	swan	swamp	swap	swab	swat	watch	swallow

_____

_____

_____

_____

_____

_____

_____

· ·

 TRACKER: Highlight the 'wa' saying '*wo*' words in the passage.

A white swan was swimming in a lake in the middle of a swamp. She wanted to swap her lonely home for a place where she could watch other creatures living their lives. She was a very sociable swan and she found the swamp rather lacking in excitement. She used her tail to swat a mosquito who was trying to be friendly. The mosquito and a wasp buzzing overhead were the only friends she was going to find that day. What a bore!

DiaPhon 2 published by Hodder & Stoughton Educational.
The publishers grant permission for photocopies of this sheet to be made for use solely in the purchasing institution.

4

'qua' saying *'quo'*

Look at the words below. Read them to yourself. Read them aloud.
Can you hear the short *'o'* sound?

quad squat squad squash

Use these words as root words and see how many more you can form
from them. You may find a dictionary helpful.

quad _____ _____ _____

squat _____ _____ _____

squad _____ _____ _____

squash _____ _____ _____

Underline the words in these sentences which use this letter cluster.

I did forty squats at the gym today and my legs hurt now.

The squadron took off early in the morning.

That is a smart squad of soldiers.

I squashed my friend when I sat on her.

Pam had quads. It was quite a shock.

An animal with four legs is a quadruped.

Look up words beginning with 'quad' in the dictionary.
What number do all the words have in common?

The number _____

Now make up sentences of your own using 'qua' words.

_____

_____

_____

_____

_____

DiaPhon 2 published by Hodder & Stoughton Educational.
The publishers grant permission for photocopies of this sheet to be made for use solely in the purchasing institution.

5

'war' saying 'wor'

Read these words aloud. Look up the meanings of any words you don't know in the dictionary or ask for help.

war	ward	warm	warn	warp	dwarf
towards	reward	wharf	swarm	swarthy	

Write a sentence for each of these words so that the meaning is clear. You can change the tense if you wish.

_____

_____

_____

_____

_____

_____

_____

_____

_____

_____

_____

_____

 TRACKER: A silly rhyme. Highlight the 'war' saying '*wor*' words in the passage.

The swarthy dwarf went down to the wharf to see if his boat had come in.

A swarm of bees followed close behind as he went towards the sea.

The sun was warm and they got their reward.

They started to make quite a din.

They buzzed and they hummed as they got the scent,

Getting some nectar was now their intent.

They forgot the dwarf and his sailing ship

And the sights that they might see.

They ate and they ate of nectar so fine.

And we all had honey for tea.

'wor' saying 'wer'

Read the words in the box to yourself, then read them aloud.
If you are unsure of the meaning of any of them, ask or look up
the word in a dictionary.

word	work	world	worth	worse
worthy	worship	worm	worthless	

Complete the sentences below with some of these words.

1. Which is worse, to _____ too hard or not to have any

    _____ to do?

2. If you _____ someone, you give them honour and respect.

3. There is a common expression: the _____ turned.

4. Complete this sequence of words. Bad, _____, worst.

5. If you are considered not to be _____ of promotion, you may

    feel _____.

• •

Now make up sentences of your own using as many of the words in the
box as you can.

_____

_____

_____

_____

_____

_____

_____

• •

Add suffixes to these words to make different parts of speech.

1. worth _____ _____

2. work _____ _____

3. worship _____ _____

DiaPhon 2 published by Hodder & Stoughton Educational.
The publishers grant permission for photocopies of this sheet to be made for use solely in the purchasing institution.

7

'al' saying 'aw'

Look at the words below. Read them to yourself. Read them aloud.

Cover the words one at a time and write them in the spaces.
Say the name of each letter as you write it. Check your spelling.

talk _____ _____ _____

walk _____ _____ _____

chalk _____ _____ _____

stalk _____ _____ _____

bald _____ _____ _____

scald _____ _____ _____

• •

Salt and *halt* are spelt with the 'al' pattern, but the sound made is that of a short 'o'. Look, say, cover, write and check.

salt _____ _____ _____

halt _____ _____ _____

• •

Answer true or false to these statements.

A bald man has lots of hair.   _____

A scald is very painful.   _____

If you halt you stop.   _____

A cabbage has a tough stalk.   _____

A small child can talk by the age of two.   _____

Chalk is black in colour.   _____

You can walk on your hands.   _____

We need some salt in our food.   _____

• •

 TRACKER: Highlight the 'al' words with the '*aw*' sound in these sentences.

People sometimes dip a celery stalk into salt before they eat it. This makes me go as white as chalk, because some doctors say salt is very bad for you. Is it all talk? I think I'll go for a walk and think about it.

'a + s' saying 'ar'

Date _____

Name _____

These words are tricky. You hear 'ar', but the words are spelt 'as':

fast	faster	last	basket	flask

TRACKER: Highlight the 'as' saying 'ar' words in the passage.
At last we were ready. The flask was in the picnic basket, the food was in little boxes, the children were in the car. It was a very fast car. We set off and flew along, going faster and faster until mum asked dad to slow down before we were stopped for speeding.

Look, say, cover, write and check these words.
Say the name of each letter as you write it.

past _____ _____

blast _____ _____

master _____ _____

fasten _____ _____

mask _____ _____

castle _____ _____

nasty _____ _____

task _____ _____

plaster _____ _____

Fill in the spaces in the sentences below using 'as' saying 'ar' words.

1. I put the picnic in the _____.

2. _____ your seat belt.

3. I broke my arm and had to have a _____ cast.

4. The _____ had towers and turrets.

5. I wore a _____ at the Halloween party.

6. A _____ of noise can damage your ears.

7. The problems are now in the _____.

DiaPhon 2 published by Hodder & Stoughton Educational.
The publishers grant permission for photocopies of this sheet to be made for use solely in the purchasing institution.

9

'a' + 'th' saying 'ar'

These words are tricky. You hear '*ar*' but the words are spelt 'ath'.

path	bath	father	rather	lather

Look, say, cover, write and check these words.
Say the name of each letter as you write it.

path   _____   _____

bath   _____   _____

father   _____   _____

rather   _____   _____

lather   _____   _____

Use these words to complete the sentences below.

1.   I like to have bubbles in my _____ when I bathe.

2.   I like to watch my _____ shaving. He looks so funny with

    _____ all over his face.

3.   The garden _____ is very long and winds from the gate to the house.

4.   Would you _____ have a cat or a dog as a pet?

Now make up your own sentences using 'a' + 'th' saying '*ar*' words.
You can use each one as often as you wish.

_____

_____

_____

_____

_____

_____

_____

'dge' words

Name_____

Read these words to yourself, then read them aloud. Ask somebody to listen to you to check if you have said them correctly. Listen for the sound of the 'd' before the soft 'g'. Look, say, cover, write and check each word in the spaces below.

badge _____   edge _____

hedge _____   bridge _____

ridge _____   lodge _____

judge _____   sludge_____

sledge_____   lodger_____

● ●

If you do not know the meaning of any of these words, ask or look them up in a dictionary. Now fit them into the sentences below.

1. I wore a _____ to show that I was a member of the team.

2. We had a _____ to stay in our spare bedroom.

3. A _____ has to make very serious decisions about the law.

4. I love to go on a _____ in the snow.

5. I went to the _____ of the cliff and looked down.

6. A dredger is a ship which is used to dredge up _____ from the river bed.

7. A _____ can be a small house at the end of the drive of a big house. The lodge keeper used to open the gates to let people in.

8. A _____ is sometimes used to divide one piece of land from another.

9. A _____ is a raised area which sticks out from the rest of the surface.

10. I had to go across a big _____ which carried the road over the top of a river.

DiaPhon 2 published by Hodder & Stoughton Educational.
The publishers grant permission for photocopies of this sheet to be made for use solely in the purchasing institution.

11

'tch' words

> The letters 'tch' make one sound. You only hear *'ch'*.
> You have to remember to put in the 't' when you write it.

Read these words aloud. Look at them carefully. Close your eyes and try to 'see' the word. Now open your eyes and look, say, cover, write and check.

match _____   patch _____

latch _____   catch _____

fetch _____   stretch _____

hutch _____   butcher _____

witch _____   kitchen _____

Now see if you can put the correct word into the spaces in these sentences. Check that the sentences make sense.

1.   Our rabbit lives in a _____ in the garden.

2.   The _____ on that door is difficult to lift up.

3.   Which _____ goes out at Halloween?

4.   Elastic is made to _____.

5.   You can buy meat from a _____.

6.   A _____ is where food is prepared.

7.   "I'm always being told to _____ and carry," said Cinderella.

8.   The pirate wore a _____ over one eye.

Adding a suffix to 'tch' – look, say, cover, write and check.

catching _____   matching _____

matched _____   clutched _____

stitching _____   snatched _____

hatched _____   bewitched _____

stretched _____   butchered _____

DiaPhon 2 published by Hodder & Stoughton Educational.
The publishers grant permission for photocopies of this sheet to be made for use solely in the purchasing institution.

12

'o' with a short 'u' sound

Name_____

 WORDSEARCH! Read the words in the box aloud. The vowel 'o' makes the sound of a short 'u'.

month	monkey	nothing	son	among	Monday	front
dozen	London	wonder	monk	wondered	wondering	

Listen to the sound of the 'o' when you say each word. Look at the spelling of the words. Try to find the words in the wordsearch.

```
m o n t h s p x v d t d x m
w s t w i n e j f c w o b o
w o n d e r e d m n i z t n
n x w o n d e r o l s e n k
t e p a i y h w t e t n e e
w o n d e r i n g l a e a y
f r o n t g t r i d b t k r
k m o n k i s o n d g w d s
a m o n g i n o t h i n g o
c w l t p n L o n d o n f q
t M o n d a y r x t t l z y
```

The words below also contain 'o' with the sound of a short 'u'. Look, say, cover, write and check them.

other _____   tongue _____   above _____

honey _____   money _____   does _____

come _____   coming _____   another _____

mother _____   brother _____   discover _____

DiaPhon 2 published by Hodder & Stoughton Educational.
The publishers grant permission for photocopies of this sheet to be made for use solely in the purchasing institution.

13

The 'v' rule

No English word ends in 'v'; there is always an 'e' after it. Sometimes the 'e' acts as a magic 'e', making the vowel in the preceding syllable say its name, not its sound – e.g. *lively*. Sometimes the letter 'o' makes the short sound of 'u' – e.g. *above*. The letter 'a' says its sound, not its name – e.g. *have*. It is all very confusing!
Things may change when you add a suffix. You may lose the 'e' but keep the same vowel sound – e.g. *love - loving*.

Read these words to yourself, then read them aloud. Ask somebody to listen to you to check if you have said them correctly. Remember we don't use the spelling 'uv', so all words with this sound are spelt 'ov' + 'e'.
Look, say, cover, write and check.

		have	live (*house*)	live (*wire*)		
love	dove	oven	above	glove	cover	discover

The letters at the end of each space tell you which letter sound or name to use. You decide whether it is a long or a short sound and write 'long' or 'short' on the line.

have	_____ *a*	live	_____ *i*
love	_____ *u*	glove	_____ *u*
cover	_____ *u*	above	_____ *u*
shovel	_____ *u*	discover	_____ *u*
oven	_____ *u*	clove	_____ *o*
dove	_____ *u*	lively	_____ *i*
drove	_____ *o*	cove	_____ *o*
stove	_____ *o*	haven	_____ *a*

Use some of the words in sentences of your own.

_____

_____

_____

_____

_____

DiaPhon 2 published by Hodder & Stoughton Educational.
The publishers grant permission for photocopies of this sheet to be made for use solely in the purchasing institution.

14

Long 'o' spelt 'ow'

Read this passage aloud, then highlight the words which are spelt 'ow' and which make the sound of a long 'o'. This is the name rather than the sound of the letter 'o'.

The archer leaned out of the narrow window. He took aim ready to fire at the distant target.

"You may miss," said his friend.

"I know I may miss," the archer replied.

"You will owe me a great deal of money if you lose the bet," his friend crowed.

"I haven't lost yet," was the low voiced answer.

At that he let loose the arrow. A great cheer was heard from the people gathered below. He could see them throwing hats in the air and dancing round in glee. Their champion had won the bet. Now they would be treated to a bowl of mulled ale and a feast of roast meats. There would be singing and dancing in the castle to celebrate the victory.

• •

Look, say, cover, write and check the words below. Notice the endings. The 'ow' doesn't change when a suffix is added.

owe _____   sown _____

slowly _____   narrowly _____

knowingly _____   mown _____

thrown _____   bowled _____

• •

Use the words to complete these sentences.

1.   The grass was _____ yesterday.

2.   The batsman was _____ out for a duck.

3.   I was _____ when the horse stopped and I didn't.

4.   The child _____ missed being run down by the car.

5.   It is a good thing not to _____ money.

6.   The seed was _____ in the spring for a summer crop.

DiaPhon 2 published by Hodder & Stoughton Educational.
The publishers grant permission for photocopies of this sheet to be made for use solely in the purchasing institution.

15

'ou' saying different sounds

> Some words don't seem to know the rules and they do their own thing.
>
> You have to learn these by heart. Look, say, cover, write and check each group of words.

Group 1 — 'ou' saying long 'oo'.

soup   _____ _____ _____

group   _____ _____ _____

coupon   _____ _____ _____

route   _____ _____ _____

routine   _____ _____ _____

through   _____ _____ _____

Group 2 — 'ou' saying long 'o'.

soul   _____ _____ _____

mould   _____ _____ _____

shoulder   _____ _____ _____

boulder   _____ _____ _____

Group 3 — 'ou' saying short 'u'.

would   _____ _____ _____

could   _____ _____ _____

should   _____ _____ _____

TRACKER: **Highlight the 'ou' words in the passage.**

The nurse told the doctor about their new patient: "The poor man changed his routine and took a different route when walking his dog. He slipped on a mouldy apple core and fell over. He has hurt his shoulder badly and I think you should see him. It would do him good if you could because it would set his mind at rest."

TRICKY 'ou' WORDS. Read them aloud.

tour   toured   tourist   pour   poured

DiaPhon 2 published by Hodder & Stoughton Educational.
The publishers grant permission for photocopies of this sheet to be made for use solely in the purchasing institution.

16

Long vowel sound
– no magic 'e'

> The words in the lists below are all spoken with a long vowel sound.
> Often, a long vowel sound is followed by an 'e', but not in these words.

Say these words aloud and listen for the long vowel sound.

bind	blind	grind	find	kind	mind	wind
pint	child	mild	wild	behind	unkind	rind
bold	cold	fold	gold	hold	sold	scold
host	most	both	almost	ghost	yolk	folk

> One word in the list is a **homograph**. This means that a word is spelt the same but is pronounced differently, depending on the meaning in a particular sentence.
> For example: **(a)** The *wind* was howling. **(b)** *Wind* up the anchor chain.
> In the first sentence the 'i' is short and we hear the *sound* of the letter; in the second the sound is long and we hear the *name* of the letter.

Look, say, cover, write and check these words.

almost _____ _____ _____

ghost _____ _____ _____

yolk _____ _____ _____

folk _____ _____ _____

Fill in the missing words in these sentences with a long vowel, short spelling word.

1. I will go and _____ my friend.

2. Put the key _____ the flower pot.

3. The _____ of a lemon is bright yellow in colour.

4. People say that silence is _____ .

 TRACKER: Highlight the no magic 'e' words in the passage.

It was a cold night but I didn't mind. I had both a scarf and gloves to keep me warm. Our host for the trip was very kind but he would scold any of us who were unable to sing because we were too cold. Yes, we were going carol singing. With luck we would receive plenty of gold for our efforts. Folk are usually very kind at this time of year.

DiaPhon 2 published by Hodder & Stoughton Educational.
The publishers grant permission for photocopies of this sheet to be made for use solely in the purchasing institution.

17

Homophones with 'ee' and 'ea'

Date

Name_____

Homophones are words which sound the same but are spelt differently, depending on the meaning.

Choose the correct word from the box to complete the sentences below.

see / sea	leek / leak	been / bean	tee / tea
week / weak	peek / peak	peel / peal	deer / dear
steel / steal	meet / meat	reed / read	beech / beach

1. I went to _____ if it was warm enough to swim in the _____.

2. The _____ is a useful vegetable which tastes rather like onion.

3. I had a _____in my bucket and all the water trickled out.

4. My sister is such a _____, she lends me her best clothes.

5. I will _____ you at six o'clock.

6. Vegetarians don't eat _____.

7. I like to _____ a book every week.

8. I was very _____ after I had a dose of flu.

9. My favourite tree is called a copper _____.

10. Have you _____ to see the new Jack and the _____ stalk pantomime?

11. I like stainless _____ pans in my kitchen.

12. The burglars planned to _____ lots of jewels.

13. You blow a _____ instrument such as a clarinet.

14. The mountain _____ was covered in snow.

15. Take a _____ at the baby and see if she is awake please.

16. I like a cup of _____ after being on the _____ at the golf club.

17. A _____ looks very beautiful when it runs across the hills.

18. Will you _____ the potatoes for me please?

19. The bell ringers rang a loud _____ before the service.

DiaPhon 2 published by Hodder & Stoughton Educational.
The publishers grant permission for photocopies of this sheet to be made for use solely in the purchasing institution.

18

Pronouncing 'ia', 'ie' and 'io' words

DiaPhon 2 Date

Name

> Usually, when you see a word with two vowels together, the first being 'i', you separate the vowels and say the sounds separately. There are exceptions though, such as 'io' in '-ion' endings and '-ie' in *sieve* or *field*.
>
> You have to learn these exceptions off by heart.

Divide these words into syllables by splitting the double vowels. Use a line to show where you make the split.

For example: onion on / i / on   furious   fur / i / ous

giant _____   brilliant _____

curious _____   carrier _____

obedient _____   riot _____

violent _____   experience _____

glorious _____   subservient _____

jovial _____   appropriate _____

radiator _____   million _____

If you say the words aloud as you spell them, breaking them into syllables, it will be easier to get the vowels in the correct order. Remember, every syllable contains a vowel. Some syllables consist of only one letter.

Decide which way round the vowels go in the unfinished words in these sentences. You will have to decide on a word which makes sense in the sentence, has the correct start and finishing letter and which has an 'i' and another vowel next to it.

1.   My mother used to tell me not to p_____t because it was rude.

2.   The Great B_____ r Reef is in Australia.

3.   A healthy d_____t will include pr_____n.

4.   The a_____e clapped the singer at the concert.

5.   I tried to ex_____n how to do the maths problem.

6.   "Stand and deliver," said the highwayman in a squeaky v_____e.

DiaPhon 2 published by Hodder & Stoughton Educational.
The publishers grant permission for photocopies of this sheet to be made for use solely in the purchasing institution.

19

Suffixing 1 – one, two, three rule

DiaPhon 2 Date _____

Name_____

> When a word has *one* vowel before a single consonant at the end of a word, double the consonant before adding a suffix such as 'ed', 'er' or 'ing'.
>
> For example: shop / shopping   run / runner.

See how many words you can form by adding suffixes to these root words.

1.   swim   _____   _____   _____

2.   win   _____   _____   _____

3.   shop   _____   _____   _____

4.   trot   _____   _____   _____

5.   clap   _____   _____   _____

6.   dig   _____   _____   _____

7.   sin   _____   _____   _____

8.   chop   _____   _____   _____

9.   chat   _____   _____   _____

10.   pat   _____   _____   _____

• •

If there are *two* vowels before the final consonant you do not need to double the consonant.

For example: clean / cleaning / cleaned   fail / failed / failure

• •

This is the one, two, three rule.

> There must be three letters, *starting with the vowel/s*, in the last syllable of the word, before you add the suffix. If there are only two, you double the consonant to make it three. There may be several consonants in front of the vowel/s, but don't include them when you count. Look at the example below.
>
>   r **u** n (n) / er   c l **e a** n / er
>   1 2 (3)   1 2 3

DiaPhon 2 published by Hodder & Stoughton Educational.
The publishers grant permission for photocopies of this sheet to be made for use solely in the purchasing institution.

20

Suffixing 2 –
words ending in magic 'e'

When a word ends in magic 'e', drop the 'e' before adding a suffix. Notice that even when you lose the 'e' you keep the magic. The vowel remains long, for example: *hope / hoped / hoping*. Sometimes an 'e' remains because it is part of the suffix, e.g. *cope / cop**ed***, or because the suffix begins with a consonant, e.g. *hope / hopeless*.

See how many words you can make by adding a suffix to the words listed below. There may be more or less than three possibilities.

save   _____   _____   _____

skate   _____   _____   _____

live   _____   _____   _____

code   _____   _____   _____

fuse   _____   _____   _____

• •

There are more difficult words ending in 'e' which behave in the same way. Try doing the same activity with these.

care   _____   _____   _____

share   _____   _____   _____

refuse   _____   _____   _____

brave   _____   _____   _____

arrive   _____   _____   _____

scare   _____   _____   _____

• •

 TRACKER: Highlight the words ending in magic 'e' in the passage.

It was freezing. Mike was happy because it was an excuse to go skating. He decided to ask his friend Kate to come as well. She was used to cold weather because she came from Norway. It was better to skate on the lake because the skating rink was too noisy.

They set off early, taking with them a picnic and a camping stove. They would need a hot drink when they had finished and the lake was in a lonely spot.

They arrived at the lake. Kate chased Mike onto the ice. There was a crack. The ice split and Mike started to sink.

"Help! I can't swim," Mike shouted.

DiaPhon 2 published by Hodder & Stoughton Educational.
The publishers grant permission for photocopies of this sheet to be made for use solely in the purchasing institution.

21

Suffixing 3 – when the suffix begins with a consonant

-ly	-ness	-ful	-s	-less	-ment	-some	-fully

When a suffix begins with a consonant and the root word ends in 'e', keep the 'e' and add the suffix.

For example: hopefully   tasteful

See how many words you can make from these root words by adding a suffix from the words in the box. You can't use all the suffixes with every word. You may need to use a dictionary.

hope	taste	hate	fate	late	safe	like	excite

_____   _____   _____

_____   _____   _____

_____   _____   _____

_____   _____   _____

_____   _____   _____

_____   _____   _____

_____   _____   _____

The same rule applies if you put two words together to make a compound word or word sum. Join together words from the two lists to form compound words. Write the words in the spaces provided. You can use a word as often as you like.

some	over	somewhere	_____	_____
book	where	notebook	_____	_____
time	what	_____	_____	_____
one	thing	_____	_____	_____
ever	table	_____	_____	_____
take	note	_____	_____	_____

Suffixing 4 – words ending in 'able'

Date _____

Name _____

> Words which usually end in 'ce' or 'ge' keep the 'e' when a suffix is added, in order for the 'c' or 'g' to remain soft when it is followed by 'a' or 'o' – for example: *manageable, courageous.*

Read these words to yourself then read them aloud to your teacher. Correct how you say them, if necessary. Now look, say, cover, write and check each one.

peaceable   _____   _____

manageable   _____   _____

changeable   _____   _____

serviceable   _____   _____

replaceable   _____   _____

· ·

> Notice that you can put prefixes on some of these words to make them mean the opposite – for example: *manageable / **un**manageable.* These are called **antonyms**. See if you can find any more of these antonyms similar to the example.

Write sentences using the words correctly.

_____

_____

_____

_____

_____

_____

_____

· ·

Soft 'g' words – look, say, cover, write and check.

orangeade   _____   _____

outrageous   _____   _____

courageous   _____   _____

DiaPhon 2 published by Hodder & Stoughton Educational.
The publishers grant permission for photocopies of this sheet to be made for use solely in the purchasing institution.

23

Suffixing 5 – words ending in 'y'

DiaPhon 2 Date _____

Name_____

We use the letter 'y' at the end of many words in English because we don't often end words with the letter 'i'. We do want the 'i' sound, though. Sometimes it is the short 'i', as in *happy* or *daisy*, and sometimes long, as in *fry* or *shy*.
When you want to add an ending to these words, you usually change the 'y' to an 'i' before you add the ending. In the box below are some of the endings we often use.

See how many new words you can make from the root words by adding the different endings. Remember, you will need to change the last letter of the root word when you add the ending.

-ly	-er	-est	-ful	-ed	-ness	-fully	-ies

pretty   _____   _____   _____

easy   _____   _____   _____

ugly   _____   _____   _____

beauty   _____   _____   _____

heavy   _____   _____   _____

busy   _____   _____   _____

carry   _____   _____   _____

reply   _____   _____   _____

There is an exception to this rule. (Well, there would be, wouldn't there!)
If the ending (suffix) begins with an 'i', you leave the 'y' alone and don't change it.
A word with double 'i' looks very odd to us.

Add *ing* to these words.

fry _____   hurry _____   reply _____

DiaPhon 2 published by Hodder & Stoughton Educational.
The publishers grant permission for photocopies of this sheet to be made for use solely in the purchasing institution.

24a

Suffixing 5 –
words ending in 'y', cont.

> The 'y' to 'i' rule does not apply when the letter before the 'y' is a vowel.
>
> For example: stay – stayed   play – played   buy – buying

Make up some sentences using the word at the beginning of each line as the root word and adding a suffix. The first one is done for you.

stay – I like staying at my grandparents' house.

play_____

_____

fray_____

_____

enjoy_____

_____

buy_____

_____

monkey_____

_____

You can see how easy it is to make up new words by adding endings to root words. Some suffixes you could use are 's', 'ing', 'ed', 'es', 'er'. How many words can you make from the following? Think carefully about the spelling of each new word. You sometimes have to change the 'y' to an 'i' before adding the suffix.

fly_____

cry_____

try_____

Suffixing 6 – words ending in 'l'

When you add a suffix to a word ending in 'l' you should:

- **double the 'l' if there is one vowel in front of it (the 123 rule).**
  For example: pedal – pedalling
  travel – travelling

- **don't double the 'l' if there are two vowels in front of it.**
  For example: fail – failing
  feel – feeling

Try to join these words and suffixes together correctly.

1. patrol + ing = _____

2. cool + ed = _____

3. shovel + ing = _____

4. marvel + ed = _____

5. appeal + ing = _____

6. feel + ing = _____

7. wheel + ed = _____

8. toil + ing = _____

9. fulfil + ing = _____

10. expel + ed = _____

Write sentences using some of these words.

_____

_____

_____

_____

_____

DiaPhon 2 published by Hodder & Stoughton Educational.
The publishers grant permission for photocopies of this sheet to be made for use solely in the purchasing institution.

25

Plurals 1 – add 's'

The usual way to form the plural (*more than one*), of a noun, is to add an 's' to the singular (*one*).

For example: table / tables book / books door / doors rose / roses.

- -

Read these sentences. Put the words in bold into the plural. Notice that you have to change more than the nouns when you use plurals.

For example:

The **dog** went mad when **he** smelt the **bone**.

The *dogs* went mad when *they* smelt the *bones*.

1. The **girl** went to buy **a new coat**.

    _____

2. The **cat was** bored on the **mat**.

    _____

3. The **dog** enjoyed eating **his bone**.

    _____

4. **I** washed **my cup** and **saucer** and put them in the **cupboard**.

    _____

5. "Put the **book** on the **table**, please".

    _____

- -

Use the words in the box to make up sentences of your own.

beds	cups	pencils	flowers	drawers	coins	boats

_____

_____

_____

_____

_____

_____

DiaPhon 2 published by Hodder & Stoughton Educational.
The publishers grant permission for photocopies of this sheet to be made for use solely in the purchasing institution.

26

Plurals 2 – add 'es'

> Nouns ending in a hissing sound spelt with 's', 'ss', 'x', or 'sh', and words which end in 'ch', form their plural by adding 'es'.
>
> For example: class / classes   tax / taxes   bus / buses   bench / benches

Read these instructions carefully.

Use the rule to help you complete the following sentences. Change the word in bold from singular to plural and write the whole word in the space provided.

1. My father complains about paying so many **tax** _____.

2. I travel to school on the **bus** _____.

3. I don't like sitting on (the) **bench** _____.

4. In summer we go to (the) **beach** _____.

5. We need six **dish** _____ and ten **glass** _____ please.

6. Do you believe in **witch** _____?

7. Are you against hunting **fox** _____?

8. **Box** _____ of **match** _____ can be dangerous.

9. Cricket **pitch** _____ need a great deal of care.

10. I decided not to go to (the) **circus** _____ again.

Now write some sentences using words which follow this rule.

_____

_____

_____

_____

_____

_____

DiaPhon 2 published by Hodder & Stoughton Educational.
The publishers grant permission for photocopies of this sheet to be made for use solely in the purchasing institution.

27

Plurals 3 – words ending in 'y'

When do you end a word with 'ys' and when with 'ies'?
You just add 's' when there is a vowel before the 'y'. A good way to remember this is to think about an easy example, e.g. *boy / boys*. All words which have a vowel before the 'y' end in the same way when you form the plural.

For example: tray / trays   monkey / monkeys   key / keys
                    toy / toys   alley / alleys

Words ending in 'y' with a consonant before the 'y' form their plurals by changing the 'y' to an 'i' and adding 'es'.

For example: penny / pennies   copy / copies   lady / ladies
                    hobby / hobbies

Use the words in the box to complete the sentences below.
Change them from singular to plural using the rule you have just learnt.

lady	alley	baby	gypsy	ecstasy	attorney
	alloy	kidney	quay	eccentricity	

1.   The _____ wore beautiful clothes.

2.   Dark _____ can be dangerous places.

3.   I don't like _____ who cry a lot.

4.   _____ often live in caravans.

5.   The girl was in _____ over her new job.

6.   Lawyers are sometimes called _____.

7.   _____ are a mixture of two or more metals.

8.   Nowadays _____ can be replaced if they fail.

9.   It is interesting to see boats tied up at the _____.

10. A person who does strange things can be said to have ecc _____.

DiaPhon 2 published by Hodder & Stoughton Educational.
The publishers grant permission for photocopies of this sheet to be made for use solely in the purchasing institution.

28

Plurals 4 – nouns ending in 'o'

Most nouns ending in 'o' come from Spanish or Italian, are musical terms, end in a double letter or are abbreviated (shortened) words. **They form their plurals by adding 's'.**

Write out the plurals of these words using look, say, cover, write and check. You may need to check the meaning of some of the words.

sombrero _____ _____ _____

poncho _____ _____ _____

disco _____ _____ _____

solo _____ _____ _____

photo _____ _____ _____

igloo _____ _____ _____

Some words ending in 'o' form their plurals by adding 'es'.

Write the plurals of these words in the spaces next to each one. Look, say, cover, write and check.

buffalo _____   mosquito _____

hero _____   potato _____

cargo _____   tomato _____

domino _____   tornado _____

echo _____   volcano _____

Change the words in bold type in the sentences from singular to plural.

1. The **buffalo**_____ were stampeding because they heard the **echo**_____ of voices in the canyon.

2. I love to eat new **potato**_____ and roast **tomato**_____.

3. The girl was looking forward to singing her **solo**_____ in the school concert.

DiaPhon 2 published by Hodder & Stoughton Educational.
The publishers grant permission for photocopies of this sheet to be made for use solely in the purchasing institution.

29

Plurals 5 – nouns ending in 'f' and 'fe'

Nouns ending in 'f' and 'fe' add 's' to form the plural. Read these words aloud. Write out each word three times using look, say, cover, write and check.

belief _____ _____ _____

roof _____ _____ _____

safe _____ _____ _____

giraffe _____ _____ _____

handkerchief _____ _____ _____

Four words can be spelt using either *-fs* or *-ves*, e.g. *hoofs / hooves*. Use whichever one you prefer to look, say, cover, write and check these words, but remember that you may see *both* forms in your reading.

hoof _____ _____ _____

turf _____ _____ _____

scarf _____ _____ _____

wharf _____ _____ _____

Some of these words may be new to you. If they are, look them up in the dictionary or ask for help. Then use the words in sentences of your own.

_____

_____

_____

_____

_____

_____

_____

_____

_____

_____

_____

DiaPhon 2 published by Hodder & Stoughton Educational.
The publishers grant permission for photocopies of this sheet to be made for use solely in the purchasing institution.

30a

Plurals 5, cont.

Some words ending in 'f' or 'fe' do not form their plurals by adding 's'.
If you listen carefully when you say the word you can hear the difference.
With these words the plural ending is -*ves*.

Practise reading these words aloud and listening to the '*ves*'.

wives   calves   elves   leaves   loaves   thieves   wolves

knives   halves   selves   sheaves   lives   themselves   shelves

You form the plural by changing the 'f' or 'fe' to 'ves'.

• •

Form the plurals of the words below and write them out in the space provided. Say the word to yourself as you write.

wife _____   calf _____

elf _____   leaf _____

loaf _____   thief _____

wolf _____   knife _____

half _____   self _____

sheaf _____   life _____

shelf _____

Use some of these words to complete the sentences.

1.   Some people say a cat has nine _____.

2.   If you cut an apple in two you will have two _____.

3.   The _____ stole all our money.

4.   The _____ of bread were rather stale.

5.   Peter put the _____ up but they fell down again.

• •

 TRACKER: **Highlight the 'ves' words in the passage.**
To catch wolves, steal like thieves in the night, armed with knives and catch
them as they try to kill calves. Take loaves of bread to eat if you get hungry. You
can wrap them in large leaves.

DiaPhon 2 published by Hodder & Stoughton Educational.
The publishers grant permission for photocopies of this sheet to be made for use solely in the purchasing institution.

30b

Plurals 6 – irregular words

With some plurals we do not add or change letters. We have a different form of the word instead. Fortunately we use most of these words often and so it is easy to learn them.

Read the words and their plural forms.
Read them aloud and write the words in the spaces provided.

	singular	plural
child / children	_____	_____
mouse / mice	_____	_____
foot / feet	_____	_____
tooth / teeth	_____	_____
sheep / sheep	_____	_____
woman / women	_____	_____
man / men	_____	_____

Start a short story using some of these words. Try to make it funny and interesting.

_____

_____

_____

_____

_____

_____

_____

_____

_____

_____

DiaPhon 2 published by Hodder & Stoughton Educational.
The publishers grant permission for photocopies of this sheet to be made for use solely in the purchasing institution.

31

'k' at the beginning of words

DiaPhon 2

Date _____

Name _____

Some words start with 'k' because if they started with 'c', the 'c' would say 's' because it is followed by 'e' or 'i':

key	king	kiss	kill	kilt	kit	kite
kid	kick	kettle	kidney	keep	kitchen	kidnap

Another group of words have the 'sc' sound but are spelt 'sk' for the same reason:

skin	skid	skiff	skill	skip	skirt	sketch

Look at the words and read them aloud.
Now write the correct word in the spaces in these sentences.

1. I lost my _____ and couldn't get into the house.

2. Put the _____ on and make us a hot drink please.

3. I fly my _____ when it is windy.

4. Steak and _____ pie is very tasty.

5. I was told to _____ quiet and not to wake the baby.

6. A _____ is usually the place where food is cooked.

7. You need a strong _____ to move a football a long way.

8. If you _____ somebody you hold them by force.

9. A Scot wears a _____ as his national costume.

10. A queen or a _____ sits on a throne.

11. 'Beauty is only _____ deep' is a popular saying.

12. A _____ is a kind of boat.

13. The car came safely out of a _____ on the ice.

14. It takes _____ to _____ a good picture.

15. Some people _____ with a rope to keep fit.

DiaPhon 2 published by Hodder & Stoughton Educational.
The publishers grant permission for photocopies of this sheet to be made for use solely in the purchasing institution.

'k' at the end of words

One-syllable words ending in a 'k' sound are spelt 'ck'. The vowel sound is short.

brick	trick	thick	flick	sick	sack	back	track
speck	truck	stuck	luck	lock	shock	flock	knock

Read the words aloud. Listen for the short vowel sound.

• •

Use the words to complete these sentences.

1.   I was _____ in the lift and couldn't get out.

2.   If you _____ pellets in class you'll be in trouble.

3.   If you win the lottery you will have had good _____.

4.   It is necessary to _____ the door when you go out.

5.   I felt _____ when I ate five chocolate bars.

6.   On Halloween night children play _____ or treat.

7.   A _____ of dust flew in my eye and made it sore.

8.   I had a _____ when I saw a ghost.

9.   A group of sheep are called a _____.

10. The word _____ has a silent 'k' at the beginning.

• •

 TRACKER: **Highlight the 'ck' words in the passage.**

It was a holiday so father decided to take us out in his new truck. We were able to go on a cart track because the truck was very strong. Mick said that he felt sick so we had to stop. We were in luck because he was able to go behind a thick bush and be sick out of sight. A flock of sheep came over to see what he was doing. He got back in the truck and we were quick to move away from him. Poor Mick, it's a bit of a shock to be sick on a day out.

• •

When you add a suffix, you still keep the 'ck'.
Look, say, cover, write and check these words.

quickly _____   luckily _____

tricky _____   backed _____

DiaPhon 2 published by Hodder & Stoughton Educational.
The publishers grant permission for photocopies of this sheet to be made for use solely in the purchasing institution.

33

Words beginning with 'j'

Read these words aloud. Listen for the 'j' sound at the beginning.
Notice that the letter after the 'j' is either 'a', 'o' or 'u'.
Cover, write and check each word in the spaces provided.

jab _____ _____	Jack _____ _____
jam _____ _____	jog _____ _____
jar _____ _____	jazz _____ _____
jump _____	jumped _____
just _____	justice _____
judge _____	judgement _____
jacket _____	jackal _____
jockey _____	jumper _____
January _____	

• •

**Read the sentence below then write sentences of your own using words
beginning with 'j'. Use a dictionary to find new words if you wish.**

The jockey put on a warm jacket because it was January and he didn't want to catch a
chill when out jumping.

_____

_____

_____

_____

_____

_____

_____

_____

_____

_____

_____

DiaPhon 2 published by Hodder & Stoughton Educational.
The publishers grant permission for photocopies of this sheet to be made for use solely in the purchasing institution.

34

Soft 'c'

> The letter 'c' says 's' when followed by 'e', 'i' or 'y'. When double 'c' – 'cc' – appears in a word, the first 'c' has a hard 'c' sound as in '*cat*' and the second says '*s*'.

Look, say, cover, write and check the words and listen for the difference in the sound of the two 'c's.

accent   _____   _____

access   _____   _____

accident   _____   _____

accidental   _____   _____

accelerate   _____   _____

success   _____   _____

successful   _____   _____

succeed   _____   _____

vaccinate   _____   _____

- -

A word we use quite often is *necessary*. Remember the spelling of this by thinking: we usually wear one collar and two socks. One 'c' and two 'ss'. Look, say, cover, write and check in the spaces provided.

necessary _____   necessarily_____

- -

TRACKER: **Highlight the soft 'c' words in the passage.**

Is it necessary to give the Prince so much attention? I know he has had an accident but the medicine seems to be working and the operation was successful. The accent must be on positive thinking.

- -

Scrambled words. Try to unscramble them. The words are all in the list at the top of the page. The first letter of each word is given.

tneacdic a_____   ccaeetarel a_____

dececus s_____   uscscse s_____

ctneac a_____   cacses a_____

Soft 'g'

The letter 'g' has a soft sound when followed by 'e', 'i' or 'y'.

> giraffe   ginger   magic   tragic   engine   gypsy   apology   energy
>
> region   gym   bandage   passage   garage   damage   village

Remember that *gypsy* can also be spelt *gipsy*.

Use some of these words to complete the sentences.

1. A _____ has a very long neck.

2. The word _____ is short for gymnasium.

3. A _____ is an area of a country.

4. _____ is a spice made from _____ root.

5. The pupil had to make an _____ for setting off a stink bomb in the classroom.

6. The nurse put a _____ on my cut leg.

7. It is a good idea to put your car into a _____ at night.

8. It takes a lot of _____ to play squash.

9. The boy was asked to pay for the _____ to the window.

10. Is a _____ larger or smaller than a hamlet?

· ·

TRACKER: Highlight the soft 'g' words in the passage.

When the boy was asked to pay for the damage to the window, he was not pleased.

"It wasn't my fault," he said. "I was minding my own business practising my magic spells. When I looked up, a giraffe was trying to look through the window. You don't expect to see giraffes in my region. It was a bit of a shock. I shouted. The giraffe jumped, banged his head and broke the window."

"I want an apology from you, not a tragic story," said his father.

More 'ar' words

Read the words in the box aloud.

cardigan	argue	argument	charming	carpenter
farther	harbour	varnish	marmalade	armour
arrive	carry	caravan	ordinary	extraordinary

Look, say, cover, write and check the words below.

cardigan _____   argue _____

argument _____   charming _____

carpenter _____   farther _____

harbour _____   varnish _____

ordinary _____   arrive _____

carried _____   armour _____

marmalade _____   extraordinary _____

Use some of these words to complete the sentences below.

1. The knight thought his new _____ was very stylish.

2. You should _____ without becoming angry.

3. The _____ about which was the best team carried on for hours.

4. Many people spread _____ on toast for breakfast.

5. The _____ comes and goes in and out of fashion.

6. The _____ was protected from the heavy seas by a breakwater.

7. Nature provides some _____ sights.

8. I _____ all the shopping home when the car broke down.

9. What time do you expect to _____ at the hotel.

10. You can use _____ to obtain a hard finish on a surface.

DiaPhon 2 published by Hodder & Stoughton Educational.
The publishers grant permission for photocopies of this sheet to be made for use solely in the purchasing institution.

37

'er' wordsearch

 WORDSEARCH! Read these words aloud. Find them in the wordsearch and highlight them.

herd	nerve	serve	verse	certain	shepherd	thunder	together
remember	passenger	number	danger	litter	water	shiver	clever
paper	remembered	worrier	river	littered	spider	temper	

```
a b g h e r d s c t h t h u n d e r
n g k o p b s e s p i d e r c x z v
e d f s a r f r n m l c l e v e r u
r v s a s h i v e r s e c a s c e c
v a b l i t t e r e d l z b r e a e
e r e m e m b e r e d i m g t w c r
t o g e t h e r b f r t y u i s z t
r e m e m b e r o b c t d f y r w a
x a c v b t e m p e r e k h d b s i
q w a t e r m f r d s r m i u w p n
s p a s s e n g e r r i v e r o i l
g n j g t y l w o r r i e r d d y
n u m b e r u i n d a n g e r v e a
l k k l s m l o y p a p e r s z r u
s h e p h e r d l m s d v e r s e l
```

Add to the root word to form different parts of speech. Discuss this with your teacher.

For example: nerve   nervous   nervousness   nervously

serve	_____	_____	_____
danger	_____	_____	_____
shiver	_____	_____	_____
thunder	_____	_____	_____
number	_____	_____	_____
offer	_____	_____	_____

DiaPhon 2 published by Hodder & Stoughton Educational.
The publishers grant permission for photocopies of this sheet to be made for use solely in the purchasing institution.

38

'au' wordsearch

DiaPhon2 Date

Name

 WORDSEARCH! Hidden in the wordsearch are 20 words containing 'au'. Find them and highlight or underline them. Tick them off in the box below when you find them. Read them aloud. If you are not sure what any of the words mean, ask or look them up in a dictionary.

aunt	because	haunt	pause	saucer	author	August
audio	audience	caught	autumn	daughter		taught
restaurant	fault	applause	haul	launch	laugh	laughter

```
t  r  a  u  d  i  e  n  c  e  i  a  t
a  s  a  u  c  e  r  h  a  u  l  p  l
u  r  a  u  t  u  m  n  c  e  t  p  a
g  e  d  a  u  g  h  t  e  r  n  l  u
h  a  u  n  t  c  l  a  u  g  h  a  n
t  r  e  s  t  a  u  r  a  n  t  u  c
l  a  u  g  h  t  e  r  i  c  k  s  h
t  b  e  c  a  u  s  e  f  y  n  e  a
x  p  a  u  s  e  c  a  u  g  h  t  u
j  f  a  u  l  t  f  a  u  d  i  o  n
A  u  g  u  s  t  a  u  t  h  o  r  t
```

Look in a dictionary for more words which begin with 'au'.
Write them on the lines below.

_____   _____   _____

_____   _____   _____

_____   _____   _____

_____   _____   _____

DiaPhon 2 published by Hodder & Stoughton Educational.
The publishers grant permission for photocopies of this sheet to be made for use solely in the purchasing institution.

39

More syllables

Every syllable contains a vowel or the letter 'y', even if the syllable is made up of only one letter, for example: *min / i / bus, happ / y*. When two vowels are together and make one sound however, we count that as one vowel, for example: *weed / ing*.

• •

In the words listed below, underline or highlight the vowel digraphs (two vowels making one sound). Think about the letter 'y'. Is it part of a digraph in any of these words? Discuss your ideas with your teacher.

sounding	louder	playing	floated	building	needed
fielding	player	faithfully	pleasurable	dangerous	

• •

Now break the words into syllables as shown in the example.

sounding   sound / ing

louder   _____

playing   _____

floated   _____

building   _____

needed   _____

fielding   _____

player   _____

faithfully   _____

pleasurable   _____

dangerous   _____

• •

Clap out the syllables in each word.
Write the number of syllables in each word in the space provided.

happening _____   escaping _____   enlargement _____

comprehensive _____   certainly _____   explained _____

expansion _____   revolution _____   interesting _____

DiaPhon 2 published by Hodder & Stoughton Educational.
The publishers grant permission for photocopies of this sheet to be made for use solely in the purchasing institution.

'll' in compound words

When you add two words together where one has a double 'l', the double 'l' often becomes single.

Look at the word sums below and copy the new word in the spaces provided.

joy + full = joyful _____ _____

un + till = until _____ _____

spoon + full = spoonful _____ _____

well + come = welcome _____ _____

all + ready = already _____ _____

all + together = altogether _____ _____

all + most = almost _____ _____

all + mighty = almighty _____ _____

Use some of these words to fill in the spaces in the sentences below.

It was almost midnight. We were waiting to give a _____
and enthusiastic _____ to the visitors when they arrived. It is the
custom in Greece to give guests a _____ of preserved fruits, rather like
jam, to show hospitality. Mother had prepared them _____. We heard a
noise. We waited _____ the knock was repeated and rushed to open the door.

More word sums with double 'l' words.
Try to make the new word, then check the spelling in a dictionary.

full / fill _____ _____

spite / full _____ _____

wish / full _____ _____

all / though _____ _____

all / ways _____ _____

DiaPhon 2 published by Hodder & Stoughton Educational.
The publishers grant permission for photocopies of this sheet to be made for use solely in the purchasing institution.

41

'll' + 'ing' and 'ed'

When you add -ing or -ed to a word ending in 'l', you should:
- **double** the 'l' if there is **one** vowel before it – e.g. *travel / travelling*.
- use a **single** 'l' if there are **two** vowels before the 'l' – e.g. *feel / feeling*.

•••

Join these root words and suffixes together correctly.

patrol + ing = _____ _____

cool + ed = _____ _____

shovel + ing = _____ _____

appeal + ing = _____ _____

feel + ing = _____ _____

wheel + ed = _____ _____

toil + ed = _____ _____

expel + ed = _____ _____

fulfil + ing = _____ _____

•••

Use some of these words to complete the sentences below.

The convicted man _____ to the judge for mercy.

I don't like _____ snow in winter.

"Have you _____ off enough to discuss the matter now?"

The boy was _____ from school.

I was not _____ very well today.

I find cooking very _____.

I enjoy _____ in the garden all day.

I had trouble _____ the supermarket trolley round corners.

The policeman was _____ his beat.

My father told me that I was _____ his dreams for me.

DiaPhon 2 published by Hodder & Stoughton Educational.
The publishers grant permission for photocopies of this sheet to be made for use solely in the purchasing institution.

42

Double letters –
two and three syllables

Two-syllable words.

cunning	**woolly**	little	**accuse**	**success**	marry
access	**account**	**quarrel**	traffic	occur	**grammar**
possess	oppose	**stubborn**	arrive	**arrest**	correct	mirror

Use a line to divide these words into syllables. Notice that the line usually splits the double letters in two – e.g. *ar / rest, cor / rect.*

• •

Complete the sentences below with the words in bold type from the box.

1. "How did you come to _____ such a weapon?" asked the police officer.

2. I put the money in my bank _____ to save for a holiday.

3. George is very _____ , once his mind is made up he won't change it.

4. The man made a citizen's _____ when he caught the burglar.

5. The goal keeper made a _____ feint to confuse the defenders.

6. You mustn't _____ someone of doing wrong unless you have proof.

7. To be a _____ at anything you must work hard.

8. The skier wore a _____ hat.

9. The correct use of language is called _____ .

10. It is a pity to _____ if you can avoid it.

• •

Three-syllable words. Look, say, cover, write and check these words.

successful _____   parallel _____

beginning _____   omitted _____

camellia _____   umbrella _____

silhouette _____   guillotine _____

disappoint _____   necessary _____

occasion _____   innocent _____

guerrilla _____   gorilla _____

DiaPhon 2 published by Hodder & Stoughton Educational.
The publishers grant permission for photocopies of this sheet to be made for use solely in the purchasing institution.

43

Double letters 2 – lly

> **Adjectives** tell us more about nouns –
>
> e.g. He was a **boastful** (adjective) **boy** (noun).
>
> **Adverbs** tell us more about verbs –
>
> e.g. He **spoke** (verb) **boastfully** (adverb) about his holiday.
>
> When an adjective ending in 'l' is changed into an adverb, double the 'l'.

Change the adjectives listed below into adverbs – e.g. *usual / usually*.

usual _____   casual _____

formal _____   careful _____

annual _____   awful _____

beautiful _____

boastful _____

successful _____

informal _____

dreadful _____

Write a sentence showing that you understand the correct use of
adjective and *adverb*.
For example: It was awfully wet today; the weather was dreadful in fact.

_____

_____

_____

_____

_____

 TRACKER: Highlight the 'll' words in the passage.
"I'm a great success," said the boy boastfully.
"Do you really think so," answered his friend carefully. "Personally I think you're
a pain."

'tion' saying 'shun'

DiaPhon 2 Date

Name

Look, say, cover, write and check the words below. Divide the words into syllables as shown in the example. Check that you understand the meaning of all the words.

For example: fiction   fic / tion

nation_____   caution _____

action _____   section _____

question _____   fraction _____

attention _____   position _____

election _____   traction _____

Use the words below in sentences of your own.

examination   multiplication   association   nationality   qualification   dictation

_____

_____

_____

_____

_____

_____

Break these words into syllables as you say, then write them.

education   ed / u / ca / tion   _____

information   _____   _____

exploration   _____   _____

exhibition   _____   _____

composition   _____   _____

reputation   _____   _____

occupation   _____   _____

conversation   _____   _____

operation   _____   _____

DiaPhon 2 published by Hodder & Stoughton Educational.
The publishers grant permission for photocopies of this sheet to be made for use solely in the purchasing institution.

45a

Look, say, cover, write and check. Divide the words into syllables the first time you write them. Say each syllable aloud as you write it the second time. For example: *att / en / tion*. Many 'tion' words are *abstract* nouns – these are names of things we know exist but can't touch or see.
Highlight any of the words below you think belong to this group of nouns. If you aren't sure, discuss with a teacher.

attention _____ _____

rejection _____ _____

injection _____ _____

direction _____ _____

addition _____ _____

collection _____ _____

correction _____ _____

prescription _____ _____

instruction _____ _____

Write down eight more three syllable 'tion' words using the clues to help you. In one word, the 'tion' is not at the end.

sol _____   el _____

pre _____   con _____

in _____   rel _____

pres _____   dic _____

Complete these sayings. Discuss them with your teacher to ensure you understand the meaning.

Necessity is the mother of _____.

It is the _____ which proves the rule.

'le' at the end of words

Look, say, cover, write and check the words below.

angle _____ single _____ jungle _____

giggle _____ stable _____ little _____

sample _____ pebble _____ middle _____

TRACKER: **Highlight the 'le' words in the passage.**

I had a terrible time today. I thought I was as fit as a fiddle but suddenly, I felt a pain in my middle. It became so bad, it was impossible to do a single thing. I was sent home from school and put to bed with a hot water bottle until the doctor arrived. The doctor made me giggle, even though I was in pain. He always, by some miracle, had a joke for all his patients. He gave my stomach a simple examination and then gave his diagnosis."It will be on to the operating table with you, my dear," he said. I gave a little sigh and fainted.

Use the 'le' words in the box to complete the sentences.

impossible	responsible	invisible	vegetable	particle	bottle
visible	throttle	battle	trouble	circle	cycle	bible

1. I am doing my best, it is _____ to do more.

2. The word _____ can mean to strangle someone, or it is the other name for an accelerator on a car.

3. The _____ of Hastings was fought in 1066.

4. I cycle round in a _____ when I get lost.

5. I was in _____ because I had not done my homework.

6. There was a _____ of dirt in my eye and it felt like a rock.

7. The teacher wanted to know who was _____ for the mess.

8. If you cannot be seen you are _____. The opposite of this word is _____.

9. I do like to eat lots of raw _____s. Perhaps I was a rabbit in a previous life.

10. The Holy _____ is usually spelt with a capital letter because it is the name of a specific book.

DiaPhon 2 published by Hodder & Stoughton Educational.
The publishers grant permission for photocopies of this sheet to be made for use solely in the purchasing institution.

46a

'le', cont.

This worksheet focuses on three-syllable words ending in 'le'.

terrible	possible	principle	probable	example
miracle	horrible	visible	sensible	obstacle

TRACKER: **Read the passage aloud and highlight the 'le' words.**

I had a terrible time getting to school today. It just wasn't possible to clear all the obstacles which life placed in my way.

The first problem arose when I over slept. The alarm clock failed to go off but by some miracle, I did wake before lunch time. I had a horrible vision of the Principal glaring at me and demanding the reason for my lateness when I arrived. I envisaged myself becoming an example to all as I was told to leave the school and never return. I dived into my clothes and grabbed my school bag which, fortunately, I always prepare at night. I looked out of the window to where the car is usually clearly visible. Not today. There was no sign of it. It had been stolen. After frantic telephone calls to the police, school and finally a taxi service, I arrived at school.

The Principal was standing on the front steps greeting a parent. I was safe for the moment.

PrincipAL means head or chief.
Write a sentence to show what *principLE* means.

_____

_____

Look, say, cover, write and check the words below.

terrible _____   sensible _____

obstacle _____   probable _____

DiaPhon 2 published by Hodder & Stoughton Educational.
The publishers grant permission for photocopies of this sheet to be made for use solely in the purchasing institution.

46b

'our' saying 'er'

Look, say, cover, write and check these words.

flavour _____   colour _____

labour _____   labourer _____

harbour _____   favour _____

humour _____   neighbour _____

honour _____   honourable _____

glamour _____   behaviour _____

vigour _____   rumour _____

journey _____   journalist _____

• •

Use 'our' words to complete these sentences. Make sure you choose the correct part of speech for the sentence. Look at spelling changes.

1. A sense of _____ is very important in a school teacher.

2. The boats sailed into _____ at sunset.

3. We are told to _____ our father and our mother in the ten commandments.

4. A _____ writes for a newspaper or magazine.

5. If you have _____ you are energetic or vigorous.

6. I love the _____ of fresh strawberries.

7. There was a _____ that the Queen was coming to town.

8. What _____ shall I paint my front door?

9. I asked my _____if they would keep an eye on my house whilst I was on holiday.

10. Planning a _____ is very interesting and exciting.

11. Poor _____ at football matches by a few fans gives all enthusiasts a bad name.

12. To tell lies is not _____.

DiaPhon 2 published by Hodder & Stoughton Educational.
The publishers grant permission for photocopies of this sheet to be made for use solely in the purchasing institution.

47

'ch' saying 'k'

Words which are of Greek origin and have a 'k' sound are spelt 'ch'.
Read the words in the box aloud. The 'ch' is pronounced 'k' in each of
them.

| chaos school ache stomach choir orchestra character anchor |
| chord chemist chemical chorus Christ Christmas Christian |

• •

Highlight the 'ch' saying 'k' words in the sentences.

1. It was chaos at school when the roof blew off.

2. I had the most awful stomach ache when I ate two pounds of gooseberries.

3. The choir and orchestra gave a spirited performance.

4. A rousing chorus of *Land of Hope and Glory* had the audience shouting encore.

5. The chemicals for sale at the chemist are carefully regulated.

6. The character of Father Christmas has become very commercial in recent years.

7. Christians are named after Jesus Christ.

8. The anchor held the boat in harbour during the storm.

• •

Look, say, cover, write and check these more difficult words.

technical _____   mechanical _____

chronicle _____   technology _____

technique _____   chlorine _____

scheme _____   architecture _____

psychology _____   archaeology _____

archaeologist _____   schooner _____

chrysalis _____   chromium _____

DiaPhon 2 published by Hodder & Stoughton Educational.
The publishers grant permission for photocopies of this sheet to be made for use solely in the purchasing institution.

'ch' saying 'sh'

Words which are of French origin and have a *'sh'* sound are spelt 'ch'.
Read the words in the box aloud. The 'ch' is pronounced *'sh'* in each of
them.

chef	machine	machinery	chalet	chassis	chauffeur
brochure	parachute	champagne	avalanche	moustache	

Highlight the 'ch' saying *'sh'* words in the sentences.

1. The French chef was cross because I wanted my fillet steak well cooked.

2. The machine made light work of what had been a heavy job.

3. The holiday brochure gave us an excellent idea of what was in store.

4. I am too nervous to do a parachute jump.

5. Champagne is a drink often used for celebrating special events.

6. The ski chalet was very well appointed.

7. Men used to wax their moustaches and twirl the ends into points.

8. An avalanche can be very dangerous if you are in its path.

9. The chassis of the crashed car was crushed.

10. The chauffeur wore a very smart uniform.

• •

Use these words in sentences of your own.

_____

_____

_____

_____

_____

_____

_____

_____

_____

DiaPhon 2 published by Hodder & Stoughton Educational.
The publishers grant permission for photocopies of this sheet to be made for use solely in the purchasing institution.

49

'que' saying 'k'

antique	technique	cheque	discotheque	unique
picturesque	oblique	pique	grotesque	

Use words from the box to complete these sentences. Use the dictionary to check the meaning of any you are not familiar with.

1. If a piece of furniture is very old, we say it is an _____.

2. The view from the bridge was very _____.

3. The _____ used for oil painting is different from that used for pastels.

4. If something is _____, it is the only one in the world.

5. On a computer, an _____ stroke looks like this /.

6. Something or someone who is _____ looks very ugly.

7. If you pay a bill by _____, you don't need cash.

8. Nancy slammed the door in a feeling of _____.

Use the words in your own sentences.

_____

_____

_____

_____

_____

_____

_____

_____

_____

_____

_____

DiaPhon 2 published by Hodder & Stoughton Educational.
The publishers grant permission for photocopies of this sheet to be made for use solely in the purchasing institution.

50

'ph' saying 'f'

DiaPhon 2 Date _____

Name _____

Look, say, cover, write and check these words.

geography _____   autograph _____

paragraph _____   phantom _____

pharmacy _____   pharaoh _____

sapphire _____   atmosphere _____

typhoon _____   amphibian _____

prophet _____   decipher _____

triumphant _____   emphasis _____

photograph _____

- -

Complete these sentences using 'ph' words.

1. The study of the earth's surface and physical features is called _____.

2. A colour of a _____ is blue.

3. A _____ is someone who foretells events.

4. An _____ can live on land and in water.

5. If you _____ something, you work out the meaning of a code or symbols.

6. _____ is another name for a ghost.

7. A _____ person shows that they are successful by their manner.

8. You would buy medicine from a _____.

9. A _____ is a violent hurricane in the China Seas between July and October.

10. You might ask a famous person to sign your _____ book.

11. A _____ was a ruler of ancient Egypt.

12. The _____ is heavy before a summer storm.

- -

TRACKER: Highlight the 'ph' words in the passage.

My nephew Philip is an interesting child. From an early age he has used the telephone book to look up phone numbers. He learned to sequence the alphabet and after that, his parents couldn't stop him from using his knowledge. It cost them a fortune because he kept telephoning everyone he could think of. Eventually, they bribed him to stop by offering a weekly trip to the zoo complete with elephant rides and the supervised use of the phone book once a week. He agreed provided he could have his photograph taken on the elephant. He drives a hard bargain.

DiaPhon 2 published by Hodder & Stoughton Educational.
The publishers grant permission for photocopies of this sheet to be made for use solely in the purchasing institution.

51a

'ph' saying 'f' — wordsearch

DiaPhon 2 Date

Name_____

WORDSEARCH! Hidden in the wordsearch are words containing 'ph' saying 'f'. See if you can find them.

physical	physics	telephone	orphan	graph	phrase
elephant	alphabet	hyphen	photograph	sphere	nephew

```
p h y s i c a l t n e p h e w
h l d f s g q s i s l s l u m
y u o t l l k a l p h a b e t
s m p h o t o g r a p h s l e
i p s e l e p h a n t r h i l
c b l b o r p h a n h c v c e
s g i s g x l p h r a s e k p
g x c b l k d y s d r l t r h
u z e h y p h e n t e h i s o
l v x l w n g s l o p e n p n
g r a p h n o s p h e r e d e
```

Try to write down any more words you can think of which begin with 'ph'. Write them on the lines below.

_____

_____

_____

_____

_____

_____

DiaPhon 2 published by Hodder & Stoughton Educational.
The publishers grant permission for photocopies of this sheet to be made for use solely in the purchasing institution.

51b

'gh' saying 'f'

There are a number of words in which 'gh' is pronounced 'f'.
Look, say, cover, write and check these words.

tough _____ tougher _____ toughest _____

laugh _____ laughter _____ laughed _____

rough _____ roughage _____ roughest _____

cough _____ coughed _____ coughing _____

trough _____ enough _____ rougher _____

TRACKER: Highlight the 'gh' saying 'f' words in the passage.

Cough, cough, cough. I seemed to have been coughing all night. I'd had enough of it now and needed help. I heard laughter coming from the sitting room. Typical. My parents were having a good time and didn't care that life was tough for me at the moment.

Complete the sentences below with 'gh' saying 'f' words.

1. To keep healthy, you need to eat plenty of _____.

2. A _____ is the name for a pigs' eating bowl.

3. It was the _____ sea I have ever seen. The waves were ten metres high.

4. I have had _____ to eat: I can scarcely move.

5. _____ is the best medicine of all.

TRICKY WORDS!
These words contain 'gh' but the pronunciation varies from word to word.
Use the words in sentences to show their meaning.

thoroughly   plough   dough   draught   drought

_____

_____

_____

_____

_____

DiaPhon 2 published by Hodder & Stoughton Educational.
The publishers grant permission for photocopies of this sheet to be made for use solely in the purchasing institution.

52

Prefixes and suffixes

A **prefix** is a group of letters placed at the beginning of a word. It can tell us about the meaning of the word – e.g. *hydro*electric is electricity produced from *water* power. Antonyms, or opposites, are often formed by the addition of a prefix, e.g. *common / **un**common, responsible / **ir**responsible*.

Prefixes

Look at each prefix and make whole words – from memory, using the dictionary or by asking for help. Write them in the spaces provided. Some words come from a Greek or Latin origin and help you guess at the meaning of new words.

For example: hydro- (water)   hydroelectric   hydrofoil   hydrous

centi- (*hundred*) _____ _____ _____

anti- (*against*) _____ _____ _____

retro- (*back/behind*) _____ _____ _____

super- (*beyond normal*) _____ _____ _____

sub- (*under*) _____ _____ _____

micro- (*very small*) _____ _____ _____

mega- (*huge*) _____ _____ _____

arbor- (*trees*) _____ _____ _____

Suffixes

There are fewer suffixes than prefixes. They are placed at the end of words. Read these suffixes and their meanings aloud. Look them up in the dictionary. Try to work out the meanings of the words in the box from the suffixes.

-graph (*written*)   -phobia (*horror/fear*)   -itis (*inflammation*)

-natal (*birth*)   -venous (*within veins*)   -dom (*a quality*)

| autograph | telegraph | claustrophobia | agoraphobia |
| serfdom | postnatal | intravenous | freedom |

'ie' saying long 'e'

Name _____

Look, say, cover, write and check the words below.

chief _____   thief _____

belief _____   grief _____

field _____   niece _____

relief _____   yields _____

frieze _____   besieged _____

mischief _____   _____

relieved _____   _____

handkerchief _____   _____

mantelpiece _____   _____

Check that you know the meaning of all these words before reading on.

Use some of these words to complete the sentences.

1. The _____ was caught red handed.

2. Lively children can get into _____.

3. A _____ is a band of pattern used to decorate something.

4. It is a _____ to take tight shoes off.

5. If a person _____ in battle, they surrender.

6. Catch your sneezes in a _____.

7. I was _____ to hear I had passed the examination.

8. A _____ is a sort of shelf above the fireplace.

9. The _____ of the Indians wore a feathered headdress.

10. The town was _____ by the enemy for so long the population was starving.

11. I have a strong _____ in myself.

12. Most people feel _____ when a pet dies.

DiaPhon 2 published by Hodder & Stoughton Educational.
The publishers grant permission for photocopies of this sheet to be made for use solely in the purchasing institution.

54

'ei' saying 'ay'

Look, say, cover, write and check the words below.
You choose whether to do it two or three times.

eight _____ _____ _____

weight _____ _____ _____

freight _____ _____ _____

veil _____ _____ _____

reign _____ _____ _____

rein _____ _____ _____

weigh _____ _____ _____

neighbour _____ _____ _____

• •

Put a circle around the correct word to complete each sentence. These words are *homophones*. They sound the same but are spelt differently and have different meanings.

1. How much do you way / weigh?

2. I live in the Vale / Veil of Aylesbury.

3. The rider has lost the horse's rein / reign.

4. The bride wore a long veil / vale.

5. The Queen reins / reigns in Great Britain.

6. Wait / weight for me!

7. What was the wait / weight of the turkey we ate at Christmas?

8. Show me the way / weigh to go home.

• •

Fill in the missing words.

A _____ train is used to carry goods such as coal and steel.

A _____ lives close to you.

DiaPhon 2 published by Hodder & Stoughton Educational.
The publishers grant permission for photocopies of this sheet to be made for use solely in the purchasing institution.

55

'ti'/'ci' saying 'sh'

You may need to check the meaning of some of these words. Read the words aloud. Use the words to complete the sentences. You may have to use some words more than once.

musician	politician	efficient	official	judicial	patient
patiently	patience	impatiently	special	electrician

1. The man waited _____ in the doctors surgery.

2. I had a _____ meal today because it was my birthday.

3. The meaning of _____ is something done by a court of law.

4. A _____ is someone who takes part in politics.

5. If you are treated in hospital you are a _____.

6. The _____ came to put in more socket outlets.

7. _____ is a virtue, possess it if you can.

8. An _____ document is one which comes from some authority such as H.M.I of Taxes. (What does H.M.I. stand for?)

9. A _____ is a person who plays a musical instrument.

10. If you have _____ you wait without complaining.

11. An _____ person does not waste time.

12. I waited _____ for the train to pass and the gates to open at the level crossing.

• •

Look, say, cover, write and check.

patient _____ _____

physician _____ _____

politician _____ _____

magician _____ _____

DiaPhon 2 published by Hodder & Stoughton Educational.
The publishers grant permission for photocopies of this sheet to be made for use solely in the purchasing institution.

56

'sion' saying 'shun'

There are many different spellings of the 'shun' sound. It is a good idea to practise as many words as you can with each letter string.

Look, say, cover, write and check.

occasion _____   vision _____

television _____   invasion _____

decision _____   revision _____

division _____   explosion _____

confusion _____   erosion _____

comprehension _____ _____

convulsion _____ _____

• •

Use the words to complete these sentences. Use a dictionary or ask if you are unsure of the meaning of any of them.

1. You study soil _____ in Geography.

2. The baby had a high temperature and had a _____.

3. You dress up for a special _____.

4. Why people do such things is beyond my _____.

5. I have lots of _____ to do before the exams.

6. The bride was a _____ of beauty as she walked down the aisle.

7. The _____ to abandon ship was made by the Captain.

8. My ears rang with the noise of the _____.

9. I saw a very good programme on _____.

10. The _____ of any country causes great suffering.

DiaPhon 2 published by Hodder & Stoughton Educational.
The publishers grant permission for photocopies of this sheet to be made for use solely in the purchasing institution.

57

'ssion' saying 'shun'

Underline or highlight the double 'ss' in the words below.
Look, say, cover, write and check.

discussion _____   expression _____

procession _____   mission _____

admission _____   permission _____

profession _____   possession _____

professional _____   expressionless _____

. . . .

Use the words to complete these sentences. Use a dictionary or ask if you are unsure of the meaning of any of them.

1. We had a _____ about Pupil Rights today.

2. The _____ was half a kilometre long.

3. My parents gave _____ for me to go on the trip.

4. My _____ of shock gave the game away.

5. I would like to qualify for the legal _____.

6. A _____ qualification is very useful.

7. The thief was charged with the _____ of stolen goods.

8. The price of _____ to the concert was five pounds.

9. The spy was sent on a delicate _____.

10. The accused was _____ when he was sentenced to life imprisonment.

. . . .

Use any of the target words in your own sentences.

_____

_____

_____

_____

_____

_____

DiaPhon 2 published by Hodder & Stoughton Educational.
The publishers grant permission for photocopies of this sheet to be made for use solely in the purchasing institution.

58

Short 'i'

In these words the 'i' has a short sound. It forms a syllable on its own.
Write the words out in the spaces separating each syllable as shown in
the example below. Write the next two without the syllable dividers.

million   mill / i / on   million   million

onion   _____   _____   _____

opinion   _____   _____   _____

studio   _____   _____   _____

furious   _____   _____   _____

curious   _____   _____   _____

radio   _____   _____   _____

serious   _____   _____   _____

serial   _____   _____   _____

previous   _____   _____   _____

champion   _____   _____   _____

• •

These words can be changed by adding different suffixes. See if you can
supply the correct endings for the root words to complete these
sentences.

1. He was a very (*opinion*) _____ young man.

2. (*Curious*) _____ killed the cat.

3. Who wants to be a (*million*) _____?

4. The boy pedalled (*furious*) _____ on his new bike.

5. The (*serial*) _____ of the book was very good. We looked

    forward to it every week.

6. The exams are something to be taken (*serious*) _____.

DiaPhon 2 published by Hodder & Stoughton Educational.
The publishers grant permission for photocopies of this sheet to be made for use solely in the purchasing institution.

59a

Short 'i', cont.

In these words the 'i' has a short sound. It forms a syllable on its own.
Look, say, cover, write and check each word.

companion _____ _____

various _____ _____

radiant _____ _____

superior _____ _____

inferior _____ _____

mysterious _____ _____

immediate _____ _____

brilliant _____ _____

Answer true or false to these questions.   True / False

1. An *inferior* garment is of good quality.   _____

2. If something is *immediate* you have to wait for it.   _____

3. A dog can be a good *companion*.   _____

4. A *brilliant* person is very clever.   _____

5. A *superior* room in a hotel costs more money.   _____

6. The *radiant* bride was unhappy.   _____

7. If you have various things to choose from, there is a *variety*. _____

8. Something *mysterious* is hidden and secret.   _____

Copy these sentences.

The mysterious but radiant woman asked for a superior room in the hotel. She wanted
it immediately and would take no excuses for inferior service.

_____

_____

_____

_____

DiaPhon 2 published by Hodder & Stoughton Educational.
The publishers grant permission for photocopies of this sheet to be made for use solely in the purchasing institution.

59b

'ure' words

Look, say, cover, write and check.

pure _____   sure _____

lure _____   unsure _____

impure _____   injure _____

endure _____   ensure _____

insure _____   insurance _____

failure _____   figure _____

pressure _____   procedure _____

These words use the letter string 'ture'.

picture	creature	capture	nature	future	adventure
puncture	temperature	furniture	manufacture	fracture	

Use the words in interesting sentences of your own.

_____

_____

_____

_____

_____

_____

_____

_____

_____

DiaPhon 2 published by Hodder & Stoughton Educational.
The publishers grant permission for photocopies of this sheet to be made for use solely in the purchasing institution.

60

'ery', 'ary', 'ory' endings

Read these words aloud: **dictionary, directory, nursery**. Listen to the sound of the ending. It usually sounds like 'er', whatever the spelling.
It may be a good idea to learn the words in groups. There are some 'patterns' of spellings which are helpful.
The 'ery' ending is often associated with a root word to which you add 'ery', 'ry' or 'y'. For example: *nurse / nursery.*

Follow the example to create new words.

potter _____   crock _____

grocer _____   machine _____

archer _____   flatter _____

bribe _____   jeweller _____

discover _____   refine _____

- -

Look, say, cover, write and check these words.
Say aloud the ending as it is spelt rather than as it is pronounced.

January _____   February _____

necessary _____   vocabulary _____

secondary _____   tributary _____

ordinary _____   library _____

secretary _____   primary _____

- -

Use these words to complete the sentences.

satisfactory   laboratory   memory   compulsory   directory

1.   My school report was only _____ this term.

2.   I do science experiments in the _____.

3.   I have a terrible _____. I can forget my own name.

4.   If something is _____ you have no choice.

5.   I looked up the number in the telephone _____.

DiaPhon 2 published by Hodder & Stoughton Educational.
The publishers grant permission for photocopies of this sheet to be made for use solely in the purchasing institution.

61

More homophones

Date _____

Name _____

> **Homophones** are words which sound the same but which are spelt differently and have different meanings.

- -

Read these groups of words aloud.
If you are unsure of the meaning, ask or look them up in the dictionary.

oar / or / ore	rain / rein / reign	for / fore / four	to / too / two
their / there / they're	rowed / rode / road	Di / die / dye	

Use these words to complete the statements.

1. You row a boat using an _____.

2. You use an umbrella to shelter you from _____.

3. I _____ the boat home to victory in the boat race.

4. _____ always fighting about something.

5. My friend Diane hates having her name shortened to _____.

6. The _____ was long and winding.

7. I used to _____ my hair green and pink when I was a punk.

8. I am _____ tired to go _____ the pictures.

9. They put _____ coats down over _____.

10. Miners extract _____ from the ground.

11. In the _____ of the first Queen Elizabeth, Sir Walter Raleigh was a famous courtier.

12. The rider _____ the bucking horse round the show ring.

13. The mother pushed her pretty daughter to the _____ and told the judges they must have been blind not to pick her for the leading role.

14. I had to _____ in my horse and wait when a lorry came roaring along the road, _____ risk an accident.

- -

Now check out these words.

allowed / aloud	hoarse / horse	course / coarse	passed / past
principle / principal	weather / whether	stationery / stationary	way / weigh
pedal / peddle	gait / gate	earn / urn	hear / here	cereal / serial

More homophones, cont.

There, **their** and **they're** are all pronounced the same way, but they are used in different situations:
- the **there** spelling indicates place – e.g. *Put it down **there**.*
- the **their** spelling shows possession – e.g. *They put **their** coats on.*
- **they're** is short for 'they are' – e.g. ***They're** going now.*

Fill in the gaps in these sentences using the correct spelling to fit the meaning of the sentence.

1. "Go over _____ and stand in the corner."

2. "Are _____ any poetry books on the shelves?"

3. "_____ going to school early today."

4. " Have you seen where I've put _____ lunch boxes?"

5. "_____ going to win the cup," I said.

6. "Your dinner is over _____ on the table."

7. "I think _____ going to search our bags," Mum said.

8. "The new houses will be built over _____."

9. "We will go and see if _____ open for business."

10. "_____ doing _____best, don't nag them."

11. I went to the circus and _____, before my very eyes, were the
    acrobats standing on the backs of _____horses."

12. "If _____ was some way of finding _____ lost
    luggage I would," said the baggage handler.

13. "Is _____ time to catch the plane?"

14. "I've had enough of _____tantrums," said the twins' mother.

Write some sentences of your own using *their*, *there*, and *they're*.

_____

_____

_____

DiaPhon 2 published by Hodder & Stoughton Educational.
The publishers grant permission for photocopies of this sheet to be made for use solely in the purchasing institution.

62b

Silent 'k' and 'g'

DiaPhon 2 Date _____

Name_____

Look, say, cover, write and check the words in the spaces provided.
When you read the words, the 'k' and 'g' are silent. When you spell them
it is a good idea to pronounce the 'silent' letters as you write.

knowledge _____ _____

knight _____ _____

knuckle _____ _____

knock _____ _____

kneel _____ _____

knob _____ _____

knead _____ _____

• •

Use a suitable form of the silent 'k' words above in these sentences.

1. The cook was _____ the dough for the bread.

2. I _____ at the door but nobody answered.

3. The professor is very _____ about rare plants.

4. The man was _____ for his services to industry.

5. Bare _____ fighting was popular in the 19th century.

6. It is customary to _____ when you pray in church.

7. The door _____ was made of brass.

• •

Read these words aloud.

gnash	gnat	gnaw	gnome	sign	design
resign	consignment	campaign	foreign	reign	

• •

TRACKER: Highlight the silent 'k' and 'g' words in the passage.
I had to design a new sign for the consignment of T shirts being manufactured for
the advertising campaign. The campaign was part of a big initiative to launch the
reign of a foreign Princess as a catwalk personality. It made our competitors
gnash their teeth in fury because the contract was worth so much to us.

DiaPhon 2 published by Hodder & Stoughton Educational.
The publishers grant permission for photocopies of this sheet to be made for use solely in the purchasing institution.

63

Silent 'b' and 'h'

Look, say, cover, write and check the words in the spaces provided.
When you read the words, the 'b' and 'h' are silent.

lamb _____   bomb _____

tomb _____   comb _____

crumb _____   climb _____

numb _____   dumb _____

debt _____   doubt _____

honest _____   honesty _____

hour _____   hourly _____

honour _____   honourable _____

exhaust _____   exhausted _____

doubting _____ _____

doubtful _____ _____

doubtfully _____ _____

plumber _____ _____

thumb _____ _____

· ·

Answer yes or no to these questions.

1. Is an *exhausted* person tired?   _____

2. Are there sixty minutes in an *hour*?   _____

3. Is a thief *honest*?   _____

4. Is a rich person likely to be in *debt*?   _____

· ·

Use these words in sentences of your own. You may alter the part of speech.

doubtful   tomb   honour   numb

_____

_____

_____

_____

DiaPhon 2 published by Hodder & Stoughton Educational.
The publishers grant permission for photocopies of this sheet to be made for use solely in the purchasing institution.

64

Silent 'w' and 'l' – wordsearch

DiaPhon 2 Date

Name

WORDSEARCH! Hidden in the search are words which contain silent 'w' and 'l' words. Find them and highlight or underline them. Tick them off in the box below when you find them. Read them aloud. If you are not sure what any of the words mean, ask or look them up in a dictionary.

wrap	wreck	wreckage	wrestler	write	written	wrong
answer	sword	calm	palm	half	calf	folk	yolk	walk	talk

```
a n s w e r b b b y o l k b w
m l c a l f r l w r a p g l r
w r e c k a l e e r e y f e i
s w r i t e y n f o l k l n t
s d b s k p a l m k r z s d t
i b l b s t b k n m o y f e e
c s w o r d l i g h h a l f n
a i r a o a o n t a l k l d n
l n e d w z w r o n g a n k g
m k k e d x n w r e c k a g e
q r j w r e s t l e r p a l m
```

Make new words from the list below by adding suffixes.
Check the spelling.

For example: answer   answered   answering

walk _____ _____ _____

talk _____ _____ _____

wreck _____ _____ _____

wrap _____ _____ _____

DiaPhon 2 published by Hodder & Stoughton Educational.
The publishers grant permission for photocopies of this sheet to be made for use solely in the purchasing institution.

65

Silent 'u' and 't'

When you read these words, the 'u' (group 1), and 't' (group 2), are silent.
Use the words to complete the sentences.

Group 1

build	builder	biscuit	disguise	guessed	guest
guide	guard	guilty	tongue	vague	guarantee

1. The _____ used old bricks to _____ the house.

2. The detective was in _____.

3. I was a _____ at the wedding.

4. The _____ was crisp and tasty.

5. I _____ you will enjoy this film.

6. The teacher said my answer was too _____.

7. The prisoner was found _____ by the jury.

8. The _____ took the prisoner to the cell.

9. I bit my _____ when I fell.

10. I didn't know the answer so I _____ it.

11. A travel _____ is useful in a strange country.

• •

Group 2

Use the words below in your own sentences.

castle	fasten	unfasten	listen	thistle	whistle

_____

_____

_____

_____

_____

DiaPhon 2 published by Hodder & Stoughton Educational.
The publishers grant permission for photocopies of this sheet to be made for use solely in the purchasing institution.

66

More silent letters

Date _____

Name _____

When you spell the words which end in silent 'n', it is a good idea to still pronounce the letter as you write the word, to remind yourself it is there.

Write the words in the spaces, naming each letter as you write it.

autumn _____ _____

condemn _____ _____

column _____ _____

hymn _____ _____

. . . .

With the group of words below, pronounce the silent 'c' as a hard 'c' when saying the word to yourself. It will help you to remember the spelling.

| scene | scenery | scent | science | scissors | scientist |

Use these words to complete the sentences.

1. The _____ in the play was quite long.

2. Don't allow very small children to play with _____.

3. Another word for perfume or aroma is _____.

4. I was asked to paint the _____ for the school play.

5. A _____ studies different types of _____.

6. I do like to see beautiful _____ from my window.

. . . .

Use these words in sentences of your own. You may need to use a dictionary. (You can hear the 'n' when you add a suffix to 'mn'.)

scientific   autumnal   condemnation   columnist

_____

_____

_____

_____

_____

DiaPhon 2 published by Hodder & Stoughton Educational.
The publishers grant permission for photocopies of this sheet to be made for use solely in the purchasing institution.

67

'ough' words

Read the verse below. Look at the 'ought' pattern. Think of the first letter of each word in:
Oh u great hairy tarantula. Now read this poem aloud.

I **bought** a great hairy tarantula,　　The boys all **fought** to hold it.
And **brought** it into school.　　　　The teacher ran away!
I knew that I **ought** not to,　　　　The girls all **thought** it was cuddly,
But it's not against the rule.　　　　And played with it all day.

Lesley Inchley

• •

Look, say, cover, write and check these words.

bought _____　　ought _____

fought _____　　brought _____

thought _____　　nought _____

In the poem, the 'ough' is pronounced '*or*'. Many other words using this pattern are pronounced differently. Ask your teacher to listen to you pronounce these words. The 'ough' is pronounced as a long '*o*'.

dough	though	doughnuts	although

• •

Use the words to complete these sentences.

1.　I like to eat _____ with lots of jam in them.

2.　You have to knead _____ thoroughly to make good bread.

3.　Blue is a pleasant colour _____ some people say it is cold.

4.　I like cheese even _____ it contains a lot of fat.

• •

Read these words aloud to your teacher.

bough	plough	thorough	thoroughly	rough	tough	trough

DiaPhon 2 published by Hodder & Stoughton Educational.
The publishers grant permission for photocopies of this sheet to be made for use solely in the purchasing institution.

68

More soft 'c' words

This may be your second or third worksheet on soft 'c' words, but there are a great many very useful words which use this rule. The ones you are about to work on are more difficult to read and spell than those you have encountered so far. Concentrate, and break the words into syllables to help you. Think of other letter string/sound patterns you have learnt.

Look, say, cover, write and check these words.

difference _____ _____

celebration _____ _____

century _____ _____

ceremony _____ _____

concentrate _____ _____

excellent _____ _____

experience _____ _____

exception _____ _____

innocent _____ _____

cancellation _____ _____

vaccination _____ _____

merciful _____ _____

democracy _____ _____

 TRACKER: **Highlight the soft 'c' words in the passage.**

At some stage in my education I hope to go on Work Experience. This is an excellent opportunity to learn and to get practice in skills relating to the world of work. I hope there will be a vacancy in the local hospital. By coincidence our neighbour works there and has encouraged me to think of hospital work as a career. I know it will not be in the emergency department because they need experienced staff. I once had to go for a vaccination and was fascinated by what I saw there. The decision will not rest with me though.

DiaPhon 2 published by Hodder & Stoughton Educational.
The publishers grant permission for photocopies of this sheet to be made for use solely in the purchasing institution.

69

More soft 'g' words

> Remember, when the letter 'g' is followed by 'e', 'i' or 'y', it is soft.
> The sound is similar to that which you think of when you see the letter 'j'.

Use some of these words to complete the sentences.

> engine   imagine   stranger   pigeon   tragedy   luggage   register
>
> bandage   package   hostage   advantage   average   courage   magic
>
> marriage   carriage   suggest   suggestion   apologise   magistrate

1.   The car's _____ was racing.

2.   The _____ was left at the post office.

3.   We were asked to make _____s for raising money.

4.   I had to _____ when I was rude to my friend.

5.   He was brought before a _____ and accused of stealing.

6.   We had to _____ we were walking in space.

7.   One _____ of being older is that you don't worry about having spots.

8.   A _____ is someone who is abducted and kept a prisoner in order to put pressure on others.

9.   A famous sight in Trafalgar Square, London, are the _____s.

10.   We had to collect our _____ from the conveyor belt in the airport.

11.   The teacher takes the _____ twice a day.

12.   The nurse put a _____ on the wound.

....

What is meant by the average? Give an example.

_____

_____

DiaPhon 2 published by Hodder & Stoughton Educational.
The publishers grant permission for photocopies of this sheet to be made for use solely in the purchasing institution.

70

More prefixes and suffixes

A **prefix** is a letter or syllable placed at the beginning of a word, a **suffix** comes at the end. Prefixes sometimes give an opposite meaning to the root word, for example: *responsible / **ir**responsible, important / **un**important.* If you know the meaning of prefixes/suffixes, it can help you to work out what the whole word means.

• •

See how many words you can find using each prefix in turn following the example. Add more '*anti*' words if you can. You may use a dictionary.

anti – *against or opposed to*

       antiseptic   **antifreeze**   **antidote**   **antiperspirant**   **antonym**

semi – *half*

_____

pro – *for / in favour of*

_____

un – *reversing the meaning*

_____

sub – *under*

_____

mis – *badly or wrongly*

_____

• •

Add more adjectives (describing words) which end in 'ier' or 'er' to this list. We say they are *comparative* because they compare one thing or person with one other – for example: *She was taller than her mother.*

naughtier   lonelier   prettier   _____ _____

_____ _____ _____ _____

• •

Add more adjectives ending in 'est' or 'iest' to this list. We say *superlative* when we are comparing one thing or person with more than one – for example: *She was the tallest girl in the class.*

happiest   toughest   healthiest _____ _____

_____ _____ _____ _____

DiaPhon 2 published by Hodder & Stoughton Educational.
The publishers grant permission for photocopies of this sheet to be made for use solely in the purchasing institution.

71

'ous'/'ious' words

DiaPhon 2 Date

Name

Look, say, cover, write and check these words.

humorous _____   jealous _____

generous _____   dangerous _____

courageous _____   _____

carnivorous _____   _____

coniferous _____   _____

....

Use these words to complete the sentences below (one word is used twice).

| obvious | mysterious | victorious | tedious | industrious |
| conscientious | anxious | serious | various | curious |

1. It was _____ that the _____ stranger
   was the culprit.

2. The _____ army returned to a rapturous welcome.

3. If you are _*in*_____ life will never be _____.

4. People who are _____ learn more than incurious people.

5. The parents were _____ about their son's progress.

6. I tried _____ remedies before I found a cure.

7. A _____ person works very hard.

8. A _____ crime deserves a _____ punishment.

....

Read these words aloud. Use them in your own sentences.

| atrocious | spacious | precious | unconscious | suspicious |

_____

_____

_____

_____

DiaPhon 2 published by Hodder & Stoughton Educational.
The publishers grant permission for photocopies of this sheet to be made for use solely in the purchasing institution.

72

'tial'/'cial' words

Read the words aloud. Use a dictionary to check the meanings then fill in the missing words to complete the sentences.

partially	essential	artificially	official	especially
artificial	partial	specialist	social	socially

1. The woman was registered _____ blind.

2. It is _____ that you get to the meeting on time.

3. The _____ agreed to see the patient at once.

4. The _____ flowers looked very realistic.

5. If you are _____ aware, you are interested in society.

6. My mother went to a _____ evening in the village hall.

7. I am _____ happy today because it is my birthday.

8. The Prime Minister made an _____ visit to our town.

9. The hit and run victim is only expected to make a _____ recovery. He will always be lame.

10. An _____ created lake is man-made.

• •

TRACKER: Highlight the 'tial'/'cial' words in the passage.

It was an official visit. All the people who prided themselves on being part of the social scene rushed out to buy a special outfit for the big day. It was an essential ingredient of the event. You were not socially acceptable unless you were wearing the latest fashion.

Mrs Cookson-Brown was a specialist in the field of etiquette for the event. She was also partial to a drop of champagne so, for the price of a bottle and some flattery, she would tell the newcomers how to get it right on the day.

The special guest would have been surprised and probably horrified at the heroic efforts made by some to be on the official guest list.

DiaPhon 2 published by Hodder & Stoughton Educational.
The publishers grant permission for photocopies of this sheet to be made for use solely in the purchasing institution.

73

'ance'/'ant' words

Look, say, cover, write and check the words using the spaces provided.

nuisance _____   entrance _____

attendance _____   alliance _____

ignorance _____   insurance _____

performance _____   _____

appearance _____   _____

extravagance _____   _____

acquaintance _____   _____

circumstances _____   _____

sergeant _____   lieutenant _____

elegant _____   ignorant _____

extravagant _____   _____

● ●

Answer yes or no to these questions.

1. Is an *elegant* person well dressed and groomed?   _____

2. Is *ignorance* the same as knowledge?   _____

3. Are you *extravagant*?   _____

4. Do you know an *acquaintance* well?   _____

5. Do people help each other when they have an *alliance*?   _____

6. Can you be seen at an *appearance*?   _____

● ●

Now use the remaining words in your own sentences.

_____

_____

_____

_____

_____

_____

DiaPhon 2 published by Hodder & Stoughton Educational.
The publishers grant permission for photocopies of this sheet to be made for use solely in the purchasing institution.

74

'ence'/'ent' words

Look, say, cover, write and check the words using the spaces provided.

argument _____   different _____

compliment _____   innocent _____

obedient _____   apparent _____

announcement _____   _____

accompaniment _____   _____

development _____   _____

independent _____   _____

parliament _____   _____

sufficient _____   _____

excitement _____   _____

magnificent _____   _____

Use the words in the box to complete the sentences.

| difference | convenience | conscience | intelligence | reference |

1. It made such a _____ when I practised the piano every day.

2. It was on my _____ that I had told a lie.

3. Common sense can be worth more than superior _____.

4. You may use a _____ library to research a topic

5. A public _____ is another name for a public toilet.

 TRACKER: Highlight the 'ence' / 'ent' words in the passage.
The announcement that the concert would start late was made to the accompaniment of cheers and jeers. An argument broke out between the organisers and it was apparent that something was very wrong. In the excitement, nobody noticed that the magnificent curtain was slowly rising to reveal an astonishing sight.

Tricky words

Date _____

Name _____

You may have worked on some of these words before. If you have, this will test your memory.

Look, say, cover, write and check. Break the words into syllables, look for known words within words or sound chunks to help you. Ask your teacher to listen to your pronunciation.

colleague _____ _____

colonel _____ _____

weird _____ _____

sergeant _____ _____

amateur _____ _____

leopard _____ _____

interfere _____ _____

merely _____ _____

yacht _____ _____

unnecessary _____ _____

jewellery _____ _____

diarrhoea _____ _____

catarrh _____ _____

cemetery _____ _____

pneumonia _____ _____

miscellaneous _____ _____

tyrannical _____ _____

accommodate _____ _____

 TRACKER: Highlight the 'tricky' words in the passage.

Last night I had a weird dream. It involved a sergeant by the name of Smith, his colleague, Colonel Chips, and a yacht with a leopard skin sail! The men set off for India on a voyage to recover a loot of gold jewellery. Unfortunately, when they arrived the colonel was struck with mysterious miscellaneous illnesses resulting in sickness and diarrhoea. They were forced to return home and the mission failed. The colonel was later reprimanded for taking unnecessary leave, but fortunately no one ever found the treasure he had smuggled back and hidden in the cemetery!

DiaPhon 2 published by Hodder & Stoughton Educational.
The publishers grant permission for photocopies of this sheet to be made for use solely in the purchasing institution.

76